THE

CREED OF PRESBYTERIANS

BY
Rev. EGBERT WATSON SMITH, D.D.

Fredonia Books
Amsterdam, The Netherlands

The Creed of Presbyterians

by Egbert Watson Smith

for Presbyterian Committee of Publication

ISBN: 1-4101-0898-8

Reprinted from the 1901 edition

Fredonia Books
Amsterdam, The Netherlands
http://www.fredoniabooks.com

In order to make original editions of historical works available to scholars at an economical price, this facsimile of the original edition of 1901 is reproduced from the best available copy and has been digitally enhanced to improve legibility, but the text remains unaltered to retain historical authenticity.

CONTENTS

PREFACE

THIS is not another essay on " The Five Points." Such treatises have their place and value, but they present our system, and only the anti-Arminian part of it at that, in its bones. They furnish no adequate conception of that divinely vital and exuberant Calvinism, the creator of the modern world, the mother of heroes, saints and martyrs in number without number, which history, judging the tree by its fruits, crowns as the greatest creed of Christendom.

This historic faith of the Presbyterian Church has in recent years been assailed with the most searching criticism, the most merciless caricature, the most vivid and eloquent abuse. That in this and every other conflict it will come off more than conqueror, we have no shadow of doubt.

But these assaults have not been without effect. The popular style in which they have been urged, the air of supercilious and triumphant certitude by which they have been characterized, the prominence and universal currency given them by the secular press, have produced among the Presbyterian rank and file, who have neither time nor facilities for special investigation, a vague but widespread feeling of uneasiness and apprehension.

For them this book is written; to answer their questions, to fortify their faith, to arm them with facts. It will be of possible service to all who desire a general knowledge of the nature, history and sanctions of the Presbyterian creed. The author even ventures to hope that some of our ministers may find here material with which to build up and defend the walls of our beloved Zion.

The reader who illustrates the perseverance of the saints by perusing this book to its close, will be able, I trust, to answer that question which for nearly four centuries has contributed so greatly to the gayety of ecclesiastical debate, " Is Calvinism dead? "

THE AUTHOR.

GREENSBORO, N. C., April, 1901.

Preface to the Study Class Edition

There is a large demand for a text-book on the history and doctrines of the Presbyterian Church, to be used in the Sunday Schools, Pastors' study classes, and the study classes of Young People's and Women's Societies. In casting about for such a book the Presbyterian Committee of Publication found ready at home that charming little book "The Creed of Presbyterians," by the Rev. Egbert Watson Smith, D. D., Executive Secretary of Foreign Missions of the Presbyterian Church in the United States. It is worthy of note that this book has already had a far larger circulation than any other book ever written in America on Presbyterianism. However, "The Creed of Presbyterians" is written in popular style for the general reader and was not primarily intended for a text-book, but the Committee of Publication hit upon a happy idea, and that was to convert it into a text-book by dividing it into lessons and adding a list of questions to be used in connection with each lesson. So we have in this new edition a book which has all the charm of the original edition and which can be read without any thought of the class-

room, but at the same time a book which
can be instantly converted into a text-book,
by turning to the lesson divisions and questions in the back. With this new adjust-
ment we believe that "The Creed of Presbyterians" will meet in an admirable way
the demand for a text-book on the history
and doctrines of the Presbyterian Church.

Practically every question on each lesson
can be answered by a careful study of the
pages assigned to that lesson, and it is not
necessary for members of the class to have
any other book in connection with the
course. But it will be found helpful to
make frequent reference to encyclopedia
articles and to such histories as members of
the class may have. It will also be found
helpful to have at hand an exceedingly interesting and informing book entitled, "The
Burning Bush: A Story of the Presbyterian Church," by J. R. Fleming. With
these suggestions we send "The Creed of
Presbyterians" out upon its new mission as
a text-book with the sincere hope and conviction that it will fill a long felt need.
The questions were prepared by Rev. W. L.
Lingle, D. D., of Union Theological Seminary, Moderator of the General Assembly of
1920.

Presbyterian Committee of Publication
Richmond, Va.

I

THE CREED FORMULATED

The Presbyterian Church has been the *The martyr* martyr Church of history. Though sword *Church.* and fagot are laid aside, she maintains her martyr pre-eminence by continuing to elicit a peculiar hostility. In popular novels, sensational sermons, and the secular press she is made the target of attack. As an acute observer has truly said, "Every heresy in doctrine or morals works itself first or last into a frenzy against Calvinism."

The persistence of these attacks renders *The need of* it important that Presbyterians should in- *the hour.* form themselves of the scriptural warrant and splendid history [1] of that great system

[1] "We love you for your glorious history." Greet-

of doctrine held by their Church, that they may be able to vindicate God's truth against error and give a reason for the faith that is in them. While we are not the only ecclesiastical body that holds this system, yet none will deny that friends and foes alike award to the Presbyterian Church, as its wreath of thorns, or its diadem of glory, the distinction of being the world's historic and leading representative of the creed of Calvinism. In this coronation we rejoice, and we would gladly attribute it to the purity in which we hold this " faith once de-livered to the saints ", and the unflinching fidelity with which in every age we have been ready to champion and to die for it.

Our creed and Calvin Our doctrinal system is known as Cal-vinism, not because it originated with Cal-vin, but because Calvin, after Paul and pos-sibly Augustine, was its ablest expounder. Misled by the name, our critics have long been in the habit of quoting as part of

ing of the Methodist Ecumenical Conference to the Pan-Presbyterian Alliance, 1892.

our faith any and every view held by Calvin. Calvin's beliefs, however, form no part of our creed except in so far as they are incorporated in our Standards, which were framed nearly a century after Calvin's death.

The doctrinal Standards of our Church *Our doc-*
are three: the Westminster Shorter Cate- *trinal Stand-*
chism, the Westminster Larger Catechism, *ards.*
and the Westminster Confession of Faith. They are not three creeds. They are three statements, varying in form, fulness, and purpose, of one and the same creed. Each is complete in itself. Each contains all the essential truths of Scripture. Each is a complete epitome of the Calvinistic system. Whoever intelligently accepts the teachings of the Shorter Catechism is a true Calvinist. Should he extend his studies to the Larger Catechism and the Confession of Faith he would find in them the same system of doctrine with which the briefer statements of the Shorter Catechism had already acquainted him.

*The Stand-
ards and
Church mem-
bership.*

Her doctrinal system the Presbyterian Church accentuates. She is pronouncedly and pre-eminently a doctrinal church. Yet the acceptance of her Standards she never requires of any applicant for admission to her fold. Her only condition of church membership is a credible profession of faith in Christ. Calvinistic and Arminian believers in Christ she welcomes with equal heartiness. Her door of entrance is wide as the gate of heaven.

*The Stand-
ards and
Office-bear-
ers.*

But of her office-bearers she requires doctrinal soundness. The question asked them at ordination is, " Do you sincerely receive and adopt the Confession of Faith and the Catechisms of our Church as containing the system of doctrine taught in the Holy Scriptures? " This formula of subscription is liberal. It binds only to " all the essential and necessary articles."[1] "The use of the words ' system of doctrine ' in the terms of subscription precludes the

---

[1] Adopting Act of 1729.

14

idea of the necessary acceptance of every statement in the Standards by the subscribers, but involves the acceptance of so much as is vital to the system as a whole."[2]

Our doctrinal formularies are known as the Westminster Standards because the famous Assembly of divines that framed them held their sessions in England's great Abbey of Westminster. Their labors extended over five and a half years, during which time they held nearly twelve hundred sessions. They met in 1643, at a period in the world's history when the human intellect, for reasons known to scholars, appears to have reached the zenith of its power. The era of the Westminster Assembly was the era of Shakespeare,[3] whose work stands matchless among the creations of the human imagination. It

Name and era

---

[2] Southern General Assembly's answer to overture of inquiry. Minutes of 1898, p. 223.

[3] Collier dates the close of the Elizabethan Era at 1659, Saintsbury and Thomas Arnold at 1660.

was the era of the translators of the English Bible, whose version remains the unapproachable model of the world's prose. It was the era of Francis Bacon, the author of the most epoch-making work in the history of human philosophy. In its own realm of theology, the work of the Westminster divines, for comprehensive grasp of Scripture truth, for clearness, compactness, and power of statement, is worthy a place beside these three other products of the human intellect at its flood-tide.

Personnel. The Westminster Assembly was a representative body, called by the English Parliament, made up of one hundred and twenty-one divines, eleven lords, twenty commoners, from all the counties of England and the Universities of Oxford and Cambridge, with seven Commissioners from Scotland. Many of them jeopardized their livings by accepting the Parliament's appointment, and after the Restoration cheerfully sacrificed their earthly all for conscience' sake. It was an elect assem-

bly. On every side were men conspicuous
for learning, eloquence, and piety; professors not only of the sacred but also of
the secular sciences; Deans, Masters, and
Heads of Colleges, Vice-Chancellors in the
great Universities. Their Moderator was
Dr. Twisse, scholar and theologian of continental fame, whose ruling passion may be
inferred from his death-bed utterance,
" Now, at length, I shall have leisure to
follow my studies to all eternity."

Nor were they scholars and theologians
alone. Amongst them were thinkers of various type—orators, statesmen, hymnists,
saints, men in every way qualified to voice
the deepest religious convictions and em-
body in symbols and institutions the intense
life of that marvellous spiritual revival
which produced "statesmen like Hampden, soldiers like Cromwell, poets like Milton, preachers like Howe, theologians like
Owen, dreamers like Bunyan, hymnists like
Watts, commentators like Henry, saints
like Baxter."

17

Milton, though not a member of the Assembly, pronounced it a " select assembly ", "of so much piety and wisdom", a "learned and memorable synod ", in which " piety, learning, and prudence were housed ".

The famous saint and scholar, Richard Baxter, author of " The Saints' Everlasting Rest", had every reason to be impartial. He wrote: "The divines there congregated were men of eminent learning, godliness, ministerial abilities, and fidelity; and being not worthy to be one of them myself, I may the more freely speak the truth, which I know, even in the face of malice and envy, that as far as I am able to judge by the information of all history of that kind, and by any other evidences left us, the Christian world, since the days of the Apostles, had never a synod of more excellent divines."

Philip Schaff, the great church historian, pronounces the above a " just tribute " to the Westminster Assembly, and says: " Whether we look at the extent or ability of its labors, or its influence upon future generations, it stands first among Protestant Councils."

The celebrated Dean Stanley, of the English Episcopal Church, declares that of all Protestant Confessions the Westminster Confession "exhibits far more depth of theological insight than any other".

The late Dr. Curry, the eminent editor of the " Methodist Advocate " of New York, in an editorial on Creeds, calls " the Westminster Confession the ablest, clearest, and most comprehensive system of Christian doctrine ever framed—a wonderful monument of the intellectual greatness of its framers ".

The Assembly had to assist them in their *Background.* work all the creeds of past ages, from the Apostles' Creed, formed in the early centuries, down to the noble Confessions and Catechisms of the Reformation period. The great Reformers, coming with fresh and eager eyes to the study of the newly opened Bible, and taking that alone as their rule of faith, were all Calvinists in theology. For the same reason the people and Church of England were Calvinistic. " The Bible ", says the historian Green, " was, as yet, the one book which was familiar to every Englishman, and everywhere its words, as they fell on ears which custom had not deadened to their force and beauty, kindled a startling enthusiasm. The whole moral effect which is produced nowadays by the religious newspaper, the tract, the essay, the missionary report, the sermon, was then produced by the Bible alone; and its effect in this way, however dispassionately we examine it, was simply amazing. The whole nation became a church. The problems of life and death, whose questionings found no answer in the higher minds of Shakespeare's day, pressed for an answer not only from noble and scholar, but from farmer and shopkeeper in the age that followed him. The answer they found was almost of necessity a Calvinistic answer." [4]

[4] " Hist. Eng. People " (American Publishers' Corporation), vol. III. p. 405.

THE CREED FORMULATED

The work before the Assembly, there- *The Assembly's task.* fore, was not the creation of a new system, but the formulation of doctrines already familiar, precious, and baptized in the blood of a hundred thousand martyrs. Its task was to give to the accepted Bible system of truth a complete, impregnable statement, to serve as a bulwark against error, as a basis of ecclesiastical fellowship and co-operation, and as a safe and effective instrument for the religious instruction of the people of God and their children.

The popular notion that the Westmin- *Ethical quality.* ster Standards consist of dry abstract dogmas, with little or no bearing upon life and duty, is a mistake. Their ethical quality is prominent and all-pervading. With them, as with the Bible, truth is in order to godliness. Nearly one half of the Confession and more than one half of both Catechisms deal directly with the practical " duty which God requires of man ". That God's holy law covers every part and particle of our lives, and that to Him we must

21

forever be accountable for our obedience or disobedience thereto, rolls like a sublime and conscience-stirring music through all the work of the Westminster divines. No other creed in existence has an article or chapter on the Divine Law comparable to that of the Confession, and nowhere else in Christian symbolism can be found such an unfolding of the heart-searching claims of that law as is given in the exposition by the two Catechisms of the Ten Commandments.

Spiritual vitality.

Whoever would understand the believer's relation to Christ and the various stages of genuine Christian experience will find in chapters xi to xviii of the Confession a presentation of that great theme unmatched by any other creed in Christendom, compact yet complete, profound yet crystallinely clear, constituting the true doctrine of the Christian life as held substantially by evangelical Christendom and the subject-matter of the best evangelical preaching of this and every preceding age.

No reference is made in our Standards to any antagonistic opinion held by any evangelical communion. Their tone is irenic. They were born, not of controversy, but of consecration. Framed " when the church was still under the happy influence of a marvellous revival, when the Word of God was felt as a living, quickening, transforming power, and preached not as a tradition, but as the very power and wisdom of God "; and " by men of ripe scholarship and devoted piety, who have remained our models of earnest preaching and our guides in practical godliness, even unto this day ",[5] they read as if every paragraph had been written in the consciousness of God's presence. Strikingly unlike many modern milk-and-water treatises on religion they undoubtedly are. Their primary appeal is not to the emotions but to the intellect. Their chief purpose is to define truth, not to apply it. Their proper

[5] "Minutes of the Sessions of the Westminster Assembly of Divines." Introduction, p. lxxv.

function is not that of a sermon or a prayer, but of a test, a testimony, a text-book. Yet so packed and throbbing are they with the vital truths of God's Word, such stress they place on personal union to Christ as the explanation of our being made partakers of the benefits of redemption, such space and prominence they give to the claims of God's moral law, that they are admirably fitted to be, as for two hundred and fifty years they have been, the spiritual food of stalwart souls, the nurse of a supremely massive and masculine type of piety.

First Characteristic. Thoroughness.

There are three things which, in addition to their character, genius, and learning, must ever commend the Westminster Assembly to our confidence. First, *the care and thoroughness with which they performed their work.*

The Catechisms.

Consider, for example, the labor expended upon the Catechisms. Catechism-making was no new work to the members of that Assembly. Theirs was an age exercised and trained beyond any previous or

24

succeeding age in the construction of doctrinal manuals. For a hundred years
Luther, Calvin, Ursinus, and a score more
of the brightest intellects of the Reformation had been devoting their best energies
to the production of catechisms for the instruction of the people. Fourteen of the
members of the Assembly were themselves
authors of excellent and widely useful catechisms. All the ripe fruits and long training, therefore, of the most catechetical century in the world's history the Assembly
had as a basis and preparation for its work.

Early in the sessions of the Assembly a *Striving*
committee of known proficients in such *after perfec-*
work was appointed to begin the undertak- *tion.*
ing. They made their report, but it was
not accepted by the Assembly. New members were added to the committee. After
much deliberation a second report was submitted. Still the Assembly was not satisfied. The committee was again changed.
After long labor a third report was presented. For three months the Assembly

had this catechism under review and discussion. It was approved almost to the
end, when again the Assembly became dis-
satisfied and determined to make a fourth
effort to secure something still nearer perfect. The committee was reconstituted
with a large addition of new members, and
was instructed to prepare two catechisms,
one larger for advanced students, and another " more easie and short for new be-
ginners ". But spite of past labors nearly
two years more of alternate report and revision were required before the last of the
catechisms was completed to the satisfac-
tion of the Assembly. The Larger was
completed first. The Shorter was not only
the last of the Catechisms, it was the last
finished work of the Assembly. In it the
Westminster divines achieved their greatest triumph. It is the consummate flower
of all their labors.

*The West-
minster vs.
other Cate-
chisms.*
Thus for five years committees of the
Assembly, and the Assembly itself, labored
upon these two little books, subjecting

every sentence, every word to the most minute and searching scrutiny. It is not too much to say that there is probably not another catechism in the world on which one tenth of the time and labor and ability and learning was expended that were employed in the production of these two with which God has so highly blessed our Church. They are the work not of one man, as Luther's and Calvin's; nor of two men, as the Heidelberg Catechism was; nor of four, as was the Catechism of the Church of Rome; but they are the product of five years of the most earnest and careful deliberations of the whole Westminster Assembly.[6]

Equal thought and care were bestowed *The mirror* upon the Confession. Every statement, *of Scripture* every alteration suggested, was examined through years of concentrated study till the entire Assembly was of one mind and fully agreed as to both doctrine and expression.

[6] "Nature and Value of the Catechisms." Strickler.

All that training the most complete and thorough, learning the most profound and extensive, intellect the most acute and searching, co-operation the most wide and helpful, labor the most intense and protracted, could do to make our Standards the perfect mirror of Scripture truth, was done.

Second characteristic, Prayerfulness.

A second leading characteristic of the Westminster Assembly was *their prayerful dependence upon God for light and guidance.*

Two traditions have come down to us, which, while of disputed authenticity, yet represent truly the spirit of prayer that pervaded the Assembly.

"More light, Lord!"

On one occasion the famous John Selden, an encyclopedic scholar and brilliant orator, addressed the Assembly to prove that excommunication was a function not of the spiritual but of the civil authority. It was a vital question involving the spiritual independence of the Church. The issue turned on the interpretation of Matt. 18 :

28

15–17. Selden's speech was subtle and powerful. It displayed a vast acquaintance with patristic and rabbinical lore. At its close the Assembly seemed to hesitate. The saintly Samuel Rutherford, who was a member, turned to George Gillespie, the youngest man in the body, and said, " Rise, George; rise up, man, and defend the right of the Lord Jesus to govern by His own laws the Church He has purchased with His blood." Thus adjured, Gillespie arose, and delivered a speech whose effect perhaps has never been surpassed. Selden's argument he utterly annihilated, proving by seven distinct lines of reasoning, all purely scriptural, that the passage in Matthew was not civil but spiritual in its import. At the conclusion of his argument Selden exclaimed, "That young man by his single speech has swept away the labors of ten years of my life." While Selden was speaking a friend had observed Gillespie apparently making notes upon the paper before him. When examined the notes proved to be only this prayer: " More light, Lord! More light, Lord!"

"What is God?" According to a familiar tradition, the Shorter Catechism's incomparable definition of God was literally born of prayer. To that great question, " What is God?" the Catechism Committee had found themselves unable to construct a satisfactory answer. The question had been referred to the Committee of the Whole. They, too, had failed. Then one of the members was called on to lead in special prayer for divine enlightenment. Rising, he thus began: " O God, Who art a Spirit, infinite, eternal, and unchangeable, in Thy being, wisdom, power, holiness, justice, goodness, and truth." When this matchless invocation fell upon their ears the Assembly felt at once that it was God's own answer, given in prayer and to prayer, descriptive of Himself.

Wrestling in prayer. Not only did the Assembly both as a body and as individuals habitually look to God for special guidance in special diffi-

30

culties, not only were the daily sessions opened and closed with prayer, but regularly every month throughout the five and a half years of its labors all business was suspended that an entire day might be given to fasting and prayer. It seems almost incredible to us that they should have remained in continuous devotional worship from morning till evening, wrestling with God often for two hours together in unbroken supplication; but in those times when all the interests of Christ's Kingdom seemed to be at stake, men realized their need of Divine help, and when once at the throne of grace knew not how to come away till the blessing was obtained. It is probably not an exaggeration to say with Dr. C. A. Briggs that "such a band of preaching and praying ministers as gathered in the Westminster Assembly the world had never seen before." No body of men ever felt more profoundly their dependence upon God, or sought more earnestly and habitually the guidance of His Spirit.

THE CREED FORMULATED

Third characteristic, Loyalty to Scripture.

The Bible and nothing but the Bible.

The third most striking characteristic of the Westminster Assembly was *their loyalty to Scripture.*

The first topic of which the Confession of Faith treats is the Divine inspiration, authority, and sufficiency of the Word of God. In its forefront stands this declaration: "The Supreme Judge, by which all controversies of religion are to be determined, and all decrees of councils, opinions of ancient writers, doctrines of men, and private spirits, are to be examined, and in whose sentence we are to rest, can be no other but the Holy Spirit speaking in the Scripture." [7]

Every member was required to take the following vow, which was read afresh every Monday morning that its solemn influence might be constantly felt: "I do seriously promise and vow, in the presence of Almighty God, that in this Assembly whereof I am a member, I will maintain nothing in

[7] Chap. I, section 10.

32

point of doctrine but what I believe to be most agreeable to the Word of God."

One of the cardinal regulations of the Assembly was in these words: "What any man undertakes to prove as necessary, he shall make good out of Scripture."

The Westminster divines were consummate masters of philosophy. They were familiar with the great schools of human thought from Plato and Aristotle down to Bacon and Descartes. But in framing these Standards their one and only aim was to express the mind of Scripture. In their whole system of doctrine no tinge of human philosophy is apparent. Says Dr. Fisher of Yale University: "One prime characteristic of Calvin's system is the steadfast consistent adoption of the Bible as the sole standard of doctrine."[8] So in our Standards there is not a paragraph which affords a hint of what philosophical school the Assembly favored. Even those questions where Scripture and

The Standards and philosophy.

[8] "The Reformation", p. 199.

philosophy intermingle were determined by the Assembly always and exclusively on biblical grounds.

The Unchanging Foundation. And herein appears the Divine wisdom by which they were guided. Human philosophies are ever changing. A system founded upon them must soon appear to totter, and to need amendment or reconstruction. " But the Word of God liveth and abideth forever." The structure which is built exclusively upon this is, like it, permanent. " In this ", declares a great Presbyterian theologian, " we find the chief glory and value of our Standards." [10] For this reason they will need radical change only when the Bible needs it.

The offense of the Word. There are hard sayings in our Standards because there are hard sayings in the Bible. Some doctrines for which the Presbyterian Church stands are among the " hard things to be understood " of which " our beloved brother Paul wrote ". " This is a hard saying, who can hear it? " So said many in

[10] " Memorial of Westminster Assembly ", p. 94.

Christ's day of Christ's teaching. They were offended. They walked no more with Him. Like many in our own day, they demanded a religion "more Christian than Christianity and more Christlike than Christ". Just so the unflinching scripturalness of our creed, its faithful mirroring of the mind of Christ revealed by His Spirit in His Word, is the reason why it never has been, is not, and never will be popular with the rationalistic and unregenerate world. "The natural man receiveth not the things of the Spirit of God." [11] The offense of the Word is as undying as the offense of the Cross.

Every statement of essential Calvinistic doctrine in our Standards the Bible substantiates by equally bold and bald statements of its own. Yet the former is the chosen object of attack. The reason is plain. In a Christian land, where the Scriptures are widely reverenced, it is cheaper and safer to assault the Presbyterian Stand-

Chief champion and martyr.

[11] I Cor. 2 : 14.

ards than to assault the Bible. Hence it is that the Presbyterian Church has always sustained the brunt of the fight for the integrity of God's truth. " We gratefully acknowledge ", said the Wesleyan Methodist Conference in its address to the Presbyterian Alliance, " the faithful and unfaltering testimony which your Church has borne throughout her entire history on behalf of the divine inspiration and authority of the Word of God." Said the Baptist Association in its greeting to the same body: " The Presbyterian Church has been the magnificent defender of the Word of God throughout the ages." Above all others, she has borne, bears now, and will continue to bear, on her name the odium, and upon her person the blows, provoked by and aimed against the Word of God. Humbly yet proudly she can say to her Lord, " The reproaches of them that reproached Thee fell on me."

Proposed revisions. Let no Presbyterian be alarmed over proposed revisions of the Confession of

36

Faith. In regard to marriage with a deceased wife's sister and the duties of civil magistrates the Confession has already been twice revised. But neither past nor proposed revisions have impaired or will impair the integrity of our Calvinistic system of doctrine.

The Revision Committee appointed in *In the Northern Church.* 1890 by the Northern Presbyterian Church brought in after two years' deliberation a report recommending twenty-eight changes in the Confession. These proposed changes, most of them very slight, involved no reconstruction of the Confessional system of doctrine. This the proposed revision would not have changed; just as the Revised Version of the Scriptures has not changed the doctrinal system contained in the Authorized Version, which, by the way, is only thirty-six years older than our Confession.

The Northern General Assembly in the spring of 1900 appointed a large committee to consider again the question of revision and report to the Assembly of 1901. Seven months later this Committee, having thoroughly examined the answers made by the Presbyteries at their fall meetings to the General Assembly's inquiry touching their attitude toward the question of revision, reported that while the returns clearly indicated that the Church desired some change in its creedal statement, either by revision, or supplemental statement, or both, yet " the returns indicate plainly that no change is desired which would in any way impair the integrity of the system of doctrine contained in the Confession of Faith."

In the Southern Church. The Southern General Assembly of 1900 was opposed to any change whatever in the Confession. It directed, however, that in future editions the following statement be printed as a foot-note to chap. x, paragraph 3: " The language of the Confession cannot by any fair interpretation be construed as teaching that any of those who die in infancy are lost." Whether the ordering by an Assembly of foot-notes to the Confession be a constitutional and wise procedure, may be questioned. As regards, however, the teaching of the Confession concerning the salvation of infants dying in infancy, the proposed foot-note clearly expresses the unanimous judgment of the highest court of the Presbyterian Church.

Amid revisional agitation the reader should never lose sight of the fact that the Confession is only one of our Standards. The Shorter Catechism, to say nothing of the Larger, is as soundly Calvinistic as the Confession, yet no revision of the Catechisms has ever been proposed or thought of. The question at issue, therefore, is not a question of orthodoxy, and no Presbyterian need be alarmed for the integrity of that historic and Scriptural system on which and for which his Church has stood from the beginning, and will surely stand to the end.

Not a question of orthodoxy.

II

THE CREED TESTED BY ITS FRUITS

By their fruits ye shall know them."—Matt. 7 : 20

II

THE CREED TESTED BY ITS FRUITS

We propose now to submit the doctrinal *The decisive test.* system incorporated in, though far older than, the Westminster Standards, to a simple yet decisive test, a test endorsed by the common sense of mankind and the authority of Christ, the test of *practical results.* In his celebrated essay on Calvinism Froude says: " The practical effect of a belief is the real test of its soundness." [1]   In His Sermon on the Mount our Lord declares, " Ye shall know them by their fruits." As a fruit-bearer, as a character-builder, as a purifying and uplifting force in the life of men and nations, how does Calvinism

[1] " Short Studies on Great Subjects ", p. 11.

rank with other doctrinal systems? We reply, it stands foremost of them all.

1. The superior moral power of Calvinism we should infer, even without the aid of history, from the inherent character and tendency of its teaching.

Calvinism and God.

It is a system distinguished supereminently by its exaltation of God. " A profound sense of the exaltation of God ", says Dr. George P. Fisher of Yale, " is the keynote of Calvinism." [2] The glory of the Lord God Almighty is its unifying all-pervading principle, the blazing sun and centre of the system. Not bare sovereignty, arbitrary will, naked power, but a personal God of grace, the God revealed in Christ, is the God of Calvinism. It adores Him as the Absolute and Ever-Blessed Sovereign, infinitely worthy of love, worship, and obedience, " Who doth uphold, direct, dispose, and govern all creatures, actions, and things, from the greatest even to the least,

[2] " The Reformation ", p. 201.

THE CREED TESTED BY ITS FRUITS

to the praise of the glory of His wisdom, power, justice, goodness, and mercy." [3] The keynote of the whole system is struck in the first question of the Shorter Catechism: "What is the chief end of man? Man's chief end is to glorify GOD, and to enjoy HIM forever." [4] " Hallowed be THY name, THY Kingdom come, THY will be done", is the threefold petition which expresses the heart of Calvinism. As one has said, "In all place, in all time, from eternity to eternity, Calvinism sees God."

From its absorbed and adoring view of God comes Calvinism's conscientiousness, *Calvinism and duty.* its deep and dominant sense of duty and responsibility. The Ever-Blessed is the Ever-

[3] "Confession of Faith", Chap. V, section 1.

[4] Said Thomas Carlyle in speaking against modern materialism: "The older I grow—and I now stand upon the brink of eternity—the more comes back to me the first sentence in the Catechism which I learned when a child, and the fuller and deeper its meaning becomes: ' What is the chief end of man ? To glorify God and to enjoy Him forever.' "

Present God, under Whose eye, in Whose fellowship, for Whose glory, and subject to Whose review, the whole of human life is to be lived. "Calvinism", says Prof. Fiske of Harvard, "leaves the individual man alone in the presence of his God." [5] Beyond all example, it intensifies man's individuality. In a clear and overpowering light it shows his responsibility to God, and his relations to eternity. Its aim is not sensation, but conviction. Feeling or no feeling, at the soul's unspeakable peril, God's commands must be obeyed; God's will must be done. Not, is it pleasant, or popular, or profitable; but, is it right? Is it what God would have me do? This is Calvinism's first question.

The Calvinist program. "Whether therefore ye eat, or drink, or whatsoever ye do, do all to the glory of God." [6] This is the Calvinistic program, illustrated in Paul, saying with his heart in his voice, "Lord, what wilt Thou have me

[5] "The Beginnings of New England", p. 58.
[6] I Cor. 10:31.

46

to do? "; in Calvin, of whom Jules Michelet says, " He felt and lived like a man before whom the whole earth disappears, and who tunes his last psalm, his whole eye fixed upon the eye of God "; in Knox, of whom Carlyle says, " The fixed centre of all his thoughts and actions was to do the will of God and tremble at nothing "; in the Puritans, whose diligence in searching the Scriptures, Green says, " sprang from their earnestness to discover a Divine will which in all things, great or small, they might implicitly obey ", in whom Taine tells us " conscience only spoke " and in whose eyes " God and duty were but one "; in the Calvinists in general, whose "system", says Henry Ward Beecher, has " no equal in intensifying to the last degree ideas of moral excellence and purity ", and whose superiority to men of other creeds, says James Russell Lowell, lies " in the prevalent sense of duty, in high ideals, in inflexible principles, in living

" 'As ever in their great Taskmaster's eye.' "

From its supreme exaltation of God springs logically and scripturally Calvinism's doctrine of sin and grace.

Calvinism and sin.

In proportion as God is great and glorious Calvinism recognizes the sin of man to be heinous and fatal. Its enormity and ill desert are beyond man's calculation or conception.[7] It is recreancy to his supreme

---

[7] " Recently a distinguished preacher of the Methodist Church remarked to me that he thought the doctrine of entire sanctification as taught by its recent advocates bore a much closer affinity to Calvinism than to Arminianism. ' How do you account for the fact', I asked, 'that it spread so readily among the Methodist churches, and can get no foothold in Presbyterian churches?' He replied that he had tried to explain the fact and had been unable. Whereupon I suggested that if the people were once indoctrinated with the Calvinistic idea of the utterly loathsome and deadly nature of sin, they could never be convinced that it was possible to get rid of it by any such easy and sudden process as that offered by the holiness brethren. He admitted that this was probably the true explanation. Undoubtedly Calvinism brands sin with a deeper infamy than any other school of theology. By as much as it emphasizes the hatefulness of sin, by so much does it emphasize the love of God, of which sinners are the object." (Reed, "The Gospel as Taught by Calvin", p. 129.)

relation. It is rebellion against the rightful authority of the Greatest and Best of beings. It is self-separation and estrangement from the Source of Truth and Life. Impenitent man is guilty, lost, "dead in trespasses and sins". Left to himself his condition is one of hopeless condemnation and misery. Thus Calvinism drags down all pride and carnal security and prostrates man at the foot of the cross, a suppliant for mercy.

In answer to his suppliant cry,[8] it reveals a salvation which is all of grace,[9] the free *Calvinism and grace.*

We supplement Dr. Reed's explanation with the remark that people who have been rightly taught in childhood "what is required" and "what is forbidden" in the Decalogue will ever after be slow to believe that any "mere man, since the fall, is able perfectly in this life to keep the commandments of God."

[8] "Whosoever shall call upon the name of the Lord shall be saved." Rom. 10 : 13.

[9] "For by grace are ye saved through faith ; and that not of yourselves ; it is the gift of God : not of works, lest any man should boast ; for we are His workmanship, created in Christ Jesus unto good works, which God hath before ordained that we should walk in them." Eph. 2 : 8, 9, 10.

49

gift of God's love and mercy in Christ.[10] In
His hands are all its blessings placed, the
Spirit of life, pardon and justifying righteousness, sanctifying, establishing, comforting, glorifying grace, resurrection, and
eternal life, and from those pierced hands
are all received. From first to last salvation is "of the Lord", of Whom, and
through Whom, and to Whom are all
things, that His may be the glory ever-
more. No inch of ground is left for human
boasting.[11] The sinner does not save himself. It is God that saves him with a salvation free,[12] present,[13] complete,[14] and everlasting.[15] He embraces the sinner in the

[10] "God, who hath saved us, and called us with an
holy calling, not according to our works, but according to His own purpose and grace which was given us
in Christ Jesus before the world began." 2 Tim. 1 : 9.

[11] "Where is boasting then? It is excluded."
Rom. 3 : 27.

[12] "The gift of God is eternal life." Rom. 6 : 23.

[13] "He that believeth on Me hath everlasting life."
John 6 : 47.

[14] "Ye are complete in Him." Col. 2 : 10.

[15] "I give unto them eternal life and they shall
never perish." John 10 : 28.

arms of unchanging love.[16] He secures him
by the bonds of an everlasting covenant.[17]
He gives him an inalienable place in the
family of God.[18] He sets before him an
unclouded prospect of final victory and
eternal joy.[19] He guarantees that all
things shall work together for his good.[20]

[16] "For I am persuaded that neither death, nor
life, nor angels, nor principalities, nor powers, nor
things present, nor things to come, nor height, nor
depth, nor any other creature, shall be able to separate us from the love of God, which is in Christ
Jesus our Lord." Rom. 8 : 38, 39.

[17] "The mountains shall depart and the hills be removed, but my kindness shall not depart from thee,
neither shall the covenant of my peace be removed,
saith the Lord that hath mercy on thee." Is. 54 : 10.

[18] "Beloved, now are we the sons of God, and it
doth not yet appear what we shall be, but we know
that when He shall appear we shall be like Him, for
we shall see Him as He is." 1 Jno. 3 : 2.

[19] "An inheritance incorruptible and undefiled, and
that fadeth not away, reserved in heaven for you who
are kept by the power of God through faith unto salvation ready to be revealed in the last time, wherein
ye greatly rejoice." 1 Pet. 1 : 4, 5, 6.

[20] "We know that all things work together for
good to them that love God, to them who are the
called according to His purpose ; for whom He did
foreknow He also did predestinate to be conformed
to the image of His Son, that He might be the first-

He shows him his name in the Book of Life, and reveals to him that he was chosen in Christ before the foundation of the world that he should be holy and without blame before Him in love.[21]   Upon his mind there breaks the amazing truth that before creation's dawn, before the morning stars sang together, or ever the sons of God shouted for joy, away back " in the beginning ", God had a thought of him, and that thought was love.[22]   Before He found a place for the universe in His hand, He had found a place for him in His heart.[23]

born among many brethren.   Moreover, whom He did predestinate, them He also called, and whom He called, them He also justified, and whom He justified, them He also glorified."   Rom. 8 : 28–30.

[21] " He hath chosen us in Christ before the foundation of the world that we should be holy and without blame before Him in love, having predestinated us unto the adoption of children by Jesus Christ to Himself."   Eph. 1 : 4, 5.

[22] " But we are bound to give thanks always to God for you, brethren beloved of the Lord, because God hath from the beginning chosen you to salvation through sanctification of the Spirit and belief of the truth."   2 Thess. 2 : 13.

[23] " Yea, I have loved thee with an everlasting love,

Thus, while Calvinism abases man as a sinner, it glorifies him in Christ as a believer, lifts him to inconceivable exaltation, commands the universe for him. His feet plucked from the horrible pit and planted on the Eternal Rock, his heart thrilled with an adoring gratitude, his soul conscious of a Divine love that will never forsake him and a Divine energy that in him and through him is working out eternal purposes of good,[24] he is girded with invincible strength. In a nobler sense than Napoleon ever dreamed, he knows himself to be a " man of destiny ". Alone among men he may be, but only more consciously allied with God. Danger may meet him, but without God's permission it cannot touch him. Death may threaten, but he is immortal till his work is done. Feeble his strength and fruitless his efforts may appear, but put forth in accordance with

" More than conqueror."

therefore with loving kindness have I drawn thee."
Jer. 31 : 3.

[24] " It is God which worketh in you both to will and to do of His good pleasure."   Phil. 2 : 13.

God's command they are the predestined means to the predestined end. Hence to his work and warfare he goes forth shielded by a panoply more invulnerable, and nerved by a courage more unconquerable, than any other faith could bestow.

2. The actual fruits of Calvinism, as set forth in history, are precisely what we should expect from the character of its doctrines.

Unequalled array of martyrs.

Calvinism has nerved more men and women to die for Christ, with thanksgiving in their hearts and psalms upon their lips, than any other creed. Its unequalled array of martyrs is one of its crowns of glory. As the Methodist Conference said, in its address to the Presbyterian Alliance of 1896: "Your Church has furnished the memorable and inspiriting spectacle, not simply of a solitary heroic soul here and there, but of generations of faithful souls ready for the sake of Christ and His truth to go cheerfully to prison and to death. This rare honor you rightly esteem as the

54

most precious part of your priceless heritage." In those centuries, when spiritual tyranny was numbering its victims by the hundreds of thousands; when in England, Scotland, Switzerland, Holland, France, men had to recant their faith or seal their testimony with their blood, nearly all the martyrs were Calvinists. Says a careful writer: " There is no other system of religion in the world which has such a glorious array of martyrs to the faith. Almost every man and woman who walked to the flames rather than deny the faith or leave a stain on conscience was the devout follower, not only and first of all of the Son of God, but also of that minister of God who made Geneva the light of Europe, John Calvin." [25]

" *Things almost supernatural.*"

The heroic moral energy inspired by Calvinism has been the admiration of historians. Motley, the famous historian of the Dutch Republic, himself allied in no way with Calvinism, declares that " the doctrine

[25] McFetridge, " Calvinism in History ", p. 113.

of predestination, the consciousness of being chosen soldiers of Christ, inspired the Puritans (Calvinists) who founded the commonwealths of England, of Holland, and of America, with a contempt of toil, danger, and death, which enabled them to accomplish things almost supernatural." [26] Its effect he describes as " that sublime enthusiasm which on either side the ocean ever confronted tyranny with dauntless front, and welcomed death on battlefield, scaffold or rack with perfect composure." [27]

" Highest glories of the human conscience."

John Morley, the eminent English author and statesman, being the adherent of no religious creed, cannot be suspected of theological bias. " Calvinism ", he says, " has inspired incomparable energy, concentration, resolution." " It has exalted its votaries to a pitch of heroic moral energy that has never been surpassed." "They have exhibited an active courage, a resolute endurance, a cheerful self-restraint, an ex-

[26] " The United Netherlands ", vol. IV. p. 548.
[27] Id.

ulting self-sacrifice, that men count among the highest glories of the human conscience." [28]

The late James Anthony Froude was one *Froude.* of England's most gifted historians and men of letters. He occupied the Chair of History at Oxford, England's greatest university. The ignorant attacks upon Calvinism which have been the fashion in recent years excited in him the scholar's just impatience. Against the inferences and misrepresentations of prejudice he set the verdict of history. From partisan logic he appealed to facts. Himself not theologically committed in any way as regards Calvinism, his impartiality is as far above suspicion as his ability and learning are beyond question.

" I am going to ask you ", says Froude, *The appeal* " to consider, if Calvinism be, as we are *to facts.* told, fatal to morality, how it came to pass that the first symptom of its operation,

[28] " Oliver Cromwell ", *The Century Magazine*, December, 1899.

wherever it established itself, was to oblit-
erate the distinction between sins and
crimes, and to make the moral law the rule
of life for States as well as persons? I shall
ask you, again, why, if it be a creed of intellectual servitude, it was able to inspire
and maintain the bravest efforts ever made
to break the yoke of unjust authority?
When all else has failed; when patriotism
has covered its face, and human courage
has broken down; when intellect has
yielded, as Gibbon says, 'with a smile or
a sigh', content to philosophize in the
closet or abroad worship with the vulgar;
when emotion, and sentiment, and tender
imaginative piety have become the hand-
maids of superstition, and have dreamt
themselves into forgetfulness that there is
any difference between lies and truth, the
slavish form of belief called Calvinism, in
one or other of its many forms, has borne
ever an inflexible front to illusion and mendacity, and has preferred rather to be
ground to powder like flint than to bend

before violence or melt under enervating temptation." [29]

"The Calvinists", says Froude, "abhorred, as no body of men ever more abhorred, all conscious mendacity, all impurity, all moral wrong of every kind so far as they could recognize it. Whatever exists at this moment in England and Scotland of conscientious fear of doing evil is the remnant of the convictions which were branded by the Calvinists into the people's hearts." [30]

As illustrating the type of character produced by Calvinism, Froude names William the Silent, Luther,[31] Knox, Andrew Melville, the Regent Murray, Coligny, Cromwell, Milton, Bunyan. "These were men", he says, "possessed of all the qualities which give nobility and grandeur to human nature—men whose life was as upright as their intellect was commanding

Type of character

[29] " Short Studies on Great Subjects ", p. 13.
[30] Id., p. 50.
[31] Luther's doctrine of Divine Grace, Sovereignty, and Predestination was thoroughly Calvinistic.

and their public aims untainted with selfishness; unalterably just where duty required them to be stern, but with the tenderness of a woman in their hearts; frank, true, cheerful, humorous, as unlike sour fanatics as it is possible to imagine any one, and able in some way to sound the keynote to which every brave and faithful heart in Europe instinctively vibrated." [32]

History vs. fiction.

With these deliberate statements of Oxford's great Professor of History, compare the representations of those popular professional story-tellers, whose only weapon is caricature, and in whose novels the Calvinistic characters are nearly all oddities, cranks, fanatics, fools, or savages.

Prejudice vs. fact.

For the enlightenment of the critics of Calvinism, Froude adds, " Grapes do not grow on bramble-bushes. Illustrious natures do not form themselves on narrow and cruel theories. Where we find a heroic life appearing as the uniform fruit of a particular mode of opinion, it is childish to

[32] " Short Studies on Great Subjects ", p. 14.

argue in the face of fact that the result ought to have been different." [33]

As a complement to the masculine illustrations cited by Froude of the Calvinistic character, we quote the following from Dr. L. P. Bowen: " Calvinism has moulded God's own type of womanhood; worth without vanity, self-sacrifice without self-righteousness, zealous service without immodesty, strong convictions without effrontery, human loveliness heightened and softened by heavenly-mindedness." " The world has never known", says an able modern scholar, " a higher type of robust and sturdy manhood, nor a gentler, purer, or more lovable womanhood, than have prevailed among those peoples who have imbibed the principles of the Calvinistic creed, with its commingled elements of granitic strength and stability, and of supreme, because Divine, tenderness and grace." [34]

Calvinistic womanhood

[33] " Short Studies on Great Subjects ", p. 14.
[34] Wilson's " Theology of Modern Literature ", p. 278.

THE CREED TESTED BY ITS FRUITS

" The best models."

To the unequalled excellence of the Calvinistic type of character, the Encyclopædia Britannica [35] bears unwilling witness. In its prejudiced article on " Predestination " it " feels bound in justice to make this remark ", that Calvinists have been " the highest honor of their own ages and the best models for imitation for every succeeding age."

"Monumental marble".

Said Henry Ward Beecher, in one of the sermons of his prime: " Men may talk as much as they please against the Calvinists and Puritans and Presbyterians, but you will find when they want to make an investment they have no objection to Calvinism or Puritanism or Presbyterianism. They know that where these systems prevail, where the doctrine of men's obligation to God and man is taught and practiced, there their capital may be safely invested." " They tell us ", he continues, " that Calvinism plies men

[35] Early edition, quoted in Smyth's " Ecclesiastical Republicanism ", p. 310.

with hammer and with chisel. It *does;* and the result is monumental marble. Other systems leave men soft and dirty; Calvinism makes them of white marble, to endure forever."

The vast knowledge and piercing insight of Thomas Carlyle none will dispute. His mature conclusion, after a lifetime of historical and biographical study, was that "Calvinism had produced in all countries in which it really dominated a definite type of character and conception of morals which was the noblest that had yet appeared in the world." [36] *"Noblest in the world."*

A review of the peoples and communities whose character Calvinism has moulded will attest the truth of Carlyle's conclusion.

IN ENGLAND.

Consider that noble body of English Calvinists whose insistence upon a purer form of worship and a purer life won for them *The English Puritans.*

[36] W. H. Lecky's "The Map of Life", 1900, p. 51.

the nickname, Puritans, " perhaps the most
remarkable body of men ", says Macaulay,
" which the world has ever produced." [37]
Out of their " impassioned Calvinism ", as
Taine describes their faith, sprang their
adoring love and reverence for God. Sovereign in right and in fact He was to them.
" To know Him, to serve Him, to enjoy
Him ", says Macaulay, " was with them the
great end of existence." [38]

> " This was all their care,
> To stand approved in sight of God, tho' worlds
> Judged them perverse."

" Their theory of life ", says Bayne, " was
that man's chief end is not to amuse or to
be amused, not to create or experience sensation, but to glorify God and to enjoy Him
forever." [39]   They were men of " celestial
purpose, of hallowed imagination, of faith
in the Unseen, the Eternal, the Divine."

The Puritan conscience. Unsympathetic and prejudiced as Taine

[37] Essay on Milton.
[38] Id.
[39] " English Puritanism." Introduction, p. 65.

64

is, a skeptic in religion, though a genius in letters and the greatest historian of English literature, he cannot but wonder at the elevation and energy of the Puritan conscience. " Strict in every duty ", he describes it, " attentive to the least requirements; disdaining the equivocations of worldly morality, inexhaustible in patience, courage, sacrifice; enthroning purity on the domestic hearth, truth in the tribunal, probity in the counting-house, and labor in the workshop." [40] In his " History of the English People ", Green marks with admiration their " implicit obedience to the Divine will alone ", their " moral grandeur ", their " manly purity ".

Army life is notoriously a school of vice. *The Puritan* It is the crucial test of morals and religion. *army.* But the Puritan army has been the wonder of the world as well for its moral purity as its invincible valor. Says Taine, " a perfect Christian made a perfect soldier." Through all that army breathed the martyr spirit of

[40] " Hist. Eng. Literature" (Alden), vol. I. p. 473.

65

their creed. Of their own accord they put their lives in jeopardy for the liberties and religion of England. Oliver Cromwell, their leader, Goldwin Smith pronounces " the greatest single force ever directed to a moral purpose ". " Upon the solid rock of Calvinistic faith ", says Morley, " Cromwell had established himself." [41] Upon the same rock his soldiers had planted themselves. The result was an army whose equal for purity and heroism the world has never seen.

" Quit you like men ; be strong."

"It never found", says Macaulay, "either in the British Islands or on the Continent, an enemy who could stand its onset. In England, Scotland, Ireland, Flanders, the Puritan warriors, often surrounded by difficulties, sometimes contending against threefold odds, not only never failed to conquer, but never failed to destroy and break in pieces whatever force was opposed to them. They at length came to regard

[41] "Cromwell", *The Century Magazine*, December 1899.

66

the day of battle as a day of certain triumph, and marched against the most renowned battalions of Europe with disdainful confidence. Even the banished Cavaliers felt an emotion of national pride when they saw a brigade of their countrymen, outnumbered by foes and abandoned by friends, drive before it in headlong rout the finest infantry of Spain, and force a passage into a counterscarp which had just been pronounced impregnable by the ablest of the Marshals of France." [42]

"But that which chiefly distinguished the army of Cromwell from other armies", says Macaulay, "was the austere morality and the fear of God which pervaded all ranks. It is acknowledged by the most zealous Royalists that, in that singular camp, no oath was heard, no drunkenness or gambling was seen, and that, during the long dominion of the soldiery, the property of the peaceable citizens and the honor of woman were held sacred. No servant girl

Chief distinction.

[42] "Hist. Eng.", vol. I. p. 119.

complained of the rough gallantry of the redcoats. Not an ounce of plate was taken from the shops of the goldsmiths." [43] Says Taine: " They raised the national morality, as they had saved the national liberty." [44]

"Tried with fire."

But a sterner test than that of war awaited the Calvinistic warriors, and a yet nobler proof they were to give of the un-rivalled strength of a Calvinistic manhood. The Protectorate having come to an end, the army was dissolved. The old veterans were turned loose to shift for themselves amid the myriad temptations of that seven-teenth century England, where beggary was a recognized and popular profession, where the police machinery even of the metrop-olis was " utterly contemptible ",[45] and where theft and robbery offered to every able-bodied man a safe and easy means of support. But though disbanded suddenly, and without resources, " they did not

[43] " Hist. Eng.", vol. I. p. 119.
[44] " Hist. Eng. Literature " (Alden). vol. I. p. 482.
[45] Macaulay's " Hist. Eng ", vol. I. p. 325.

bring ", says Taine, " a single recruit to the vagabonds and bandits." [46] " Fifty thousand veterans ", says Macaulay, " accustomed to the profession of arms, were at once thrown on the world: and experience seemed to warrant the belief that this change would produce much misery and crime, that the discharged veterans would be seen begging in every street, or that they would be driven by hunger to pillage. But no such result followed. In a few months there remained not a trace that the most formidable army in the world had just been absorbed into the mass of the community.   The Royalists themselves confessed that in every department of honest industry the discarded warriors prospered beyond other men, that none was charged with any theft or robbery, that none was heard to ask an alms, and that if a baker, a mason, or a wagoner attracted notice by his diligence and sobriety, he was in all probability one of Oliver's old soldiers." [47]

" Coming forth as gold."

[46] " Hist. Eng. Literature " (Alden), vol. I. p. 482.
[47] " Hist. Eng.", vol. I. p. 147.

Historical demonstration. The above remarkable narrative, which from first to last we have sketched as far as possible in the very words of eminent and trustworthy authors, is a striking demonstration from history of the supreme character-making power of Calvinism. The picture here presented of the character of the Puritans is in accord with the latest historical investigations. Of the two admirable lives of Cromwell issued in 1900, the able reviewer of *The Independent* says: " In both authors the Puritan character stands out towering above the age that gave it birth, and an inspiration and an ideal to all ages that follow after." [48]

" Inestimable obligations." But in producing the Puritans, Calvinism has not only proved its power, it has laid the modern world under what Macaulay rightly terms "inestimable obligations".[49] Those English Calvinists did not labor and die for themselves alone. They

---

[48] *The Independent*, Nov. 15, 1900, p. 2748.
[49] Essay on Milton.

stood in the breach for all succeeding generations.

Says Prof. John Fiske, the profoundest *Human* philosopher as he is the finest literary artist *liberty.* among the historical writers of America: " It is not too much to say that in the seventeenth century the entire political future of mankind was staked upon the questions that were at issue in England. Had it not been for the Puritans, political liberty would probably have disappeared from the world. If ever there were men who laid down their lives in the cause of all mankind, it was those grim old Ironsides, whose watch-words were texts of Holy Writ, whose battle-cries were hymns of praise."[50]

Since the Genevan reformer was " incontestably the father of the English Puritans ",[51] no man can deny the justice of Fiske's conclusion that " it would be hard to overrate the debt which mankind owe to Calvin ".

[50] " The Beginnings of New England ", pp. 37, 51.
[51] Dyer's " Modern Europe ", vol. II. p. 130.

THE CREED TESTED BY ITS FRUITS

Anglo-Saxon Protestant-ism.

But political liberty is only a part of our Puritan heritage. Says Bancroft: " That the English people became Protestant is due to the Puritans."[52] The significance of this fact is beyond computation. English Protestantism, with its open Bible, its spiritual and intellectual freedom, meant the Protestantism not only of the American colonies, but of that virile and multiplying race which for three centuries has been carrying the Anglo-Saxon language, religion, and institutions into all the world.

As the Puritans saved England to Protestantism, so the Calvinists in general saved Protestantism to the world. " Whatever was the cause ", says Froude, " the Calvinists were the only fighting Protestants. It was they whose faith gave them courage to stand up for the Reformation, and but for them the Reformation would have been crushed."

The Christian Home.

A third " inestimable obligation " we should never forget. Says Green: " Home,

[52] " Hist. U. S.", vol. I. p. 289.

72

as we conceive it now, was the creation of the Puritan." [53] In an age when woman was the slave, the idol, or the toy of man; when adultery was a jest and indecency a fashion; when even in the domestic circle the worst vices were practiced, then it was that Calvinism, by its moral purity, its sanctification of the marriage covenant as the symbol of the believer's relation to Christ, its belief in the sublime possibilities of every individual, woman and child as well as man, created out of a corrupt society that shrine of affection, that school of virtue, that radiant centre of every holy influence, the Christian Home.

Of such beneficent and lasting products *Summary* of Puritanism, Lowell might well have been thinking when he declared that " the embodiment in human institutions of truths uttered by the Son of man eighteen centuries ago was to be mainly the work of Puritan thought and Puritan self-devo-

[53] " Hist. Eng. People ", vol. III. p. 414.

tion." [54] Surely it should stop the mouths of the detractors of Calvinism to remember that from men of that creed we inherit, as the fruit of their blood and toil, their prayers and teachings, our civil liberty, our Protestant faith, our Christian homes.

Calvinism and Christian civilization.

The thoughtful reader, noting that these three blessings lie at the root of all that is best and greatest in the modern world, may be startled at the implied claim that our present Christian civilization is but the fruitage of Calvinism. Yet it is even so. The historian Green, of the Episcopal Church of England, states both the fact and its explanation when he deliberately declares: " It is in Calvinism that the modern world strikes its roots; for it was Calvinism that first revealed the worth and dignity of man." [55]

IN HOLLAND.

A bright and bloody chapter.

Another glorious chapter in the history of Calvinism and humanity, though written

[54] " Lowell's Prose Works ", vol. II. p. 2.
[55] " Hist. Eng. People ", vol. III. p. 114.

in blood, is the record of the long struggle of the Hollanders for civil and religious freedom against the gigantic power of Spain. For eighty years the strongest nation in the world labored with all its might to crush well-nigh the smallest, and failed. Says Douglas Campbell, in his massive and masterly work on " The Puritan in Holland, England, and America ": " The Puritans of Holland battled for their liberties during four fifths of a century, facing not alone the bravest and best-trained soldiers of the age, but flames, the gibbet, flood, siege, pestilence, and famine. Every atrocity that religious fanaticism could invent, every horror that ever followed in the train of war, swept over and desolated their land." [56] Holland was made a spectacle to all nations by her sufferings, and surpassed all other Christian communities in the number and steadfastness of her martyrs.[57] The

[56] Vol I. p. 133.
[57] " The Universal Cyclopedia ", Article " Calvinism ".

Duke of Alva boasted that within the short
space of five years he had delivered 18,600
heretics to the executioner. " The scaffold ", says Motley, " had its daily victims,
but did not make a single convert. . . .
There were men who dared and suffered as
much as men can dare and suffer in this
world, and for the noblest cause that can
inspire humanity." His pages picture to
us " the heroism with which men took each
other by the hand and walked into the
flames, or with which women sang a song
of triumph while the grave-digger was
shovelling the earth upon their living
faces."

A Thrilling example.

In the siege of Leyden we have a thrilling
example of their sufferings and heroism.
Three months after the commencement of
the siege the food-supply was exhausted.
A fearful famine began to rage. For seven
weeks the inhabitants had no bread to eat
and multitudes perished of hunger. On
the heels of the famine came the plague or
black death, which carried off a third part

of the citizens. The apparently doomed survivors subsisted on dogs and cats. To the summons to surrender, they replied: " As long as you hear the mew of a cat or the bark of a dog you may know that the city holds out. And when all have perished but ourselves, we will devour our left arms, retaining our right to defend our women, our liberty, and our religion against the foreign tyrant." When at last relief came they were almost starved to death. They could scarcely drag themselves along. Yet all to a man staggered or crawled as best they could to the house of prayer. There on their knees they gave thanks to God. But when they tried to utter their gratitude in psalms of praise they were almost voiceless, for there was no strength left in them, and the tones of their song died away in grateful sobbing and weeping.

In that awful and protracted struggle, *"In hoc* which Campbell pronounces "a war un- *vince."* paralleled in the history of arms", the Dutch patriots had their feet planted on

77

that rock on which Cromwell and his Ironsides in the next century established themselves—"the solid rock of Calvinistic
faith". "Calvinism", says Bancroft, himself ecclesiastically allied in no way with
that faith, "inspired Holland with a heroic
enthusiasm". None but "zealous Calvinists", as Campbell calls them, could have
suffered and endured and fought and
wrought as they did. "In the moral warfare for freedom", says Bancroft, "their
creed was a part of their army and their
most faithful ally in the battle." [58] This it
was, as Motley has already told us, that
"inspired them with a contempt for toil,
danger, and death which enabled them to
accomplish things almost supernatural."

William the Silent. The illustrious Dutch leader, William the
Silent, Prince of Orange, though reared in
another faith, was forced by the intensity
of his trials and the immensity of his re-
sponsibilities to flee to Calvinism for rest
and refuge. In its great Scripture doc-

[58] "Hist. U. S.", vol. I. p. 464.

trines of the Divine Sovereignty and Government his suffering soul found peace and strength. He became a devout Calvinist; and "from this time forth", says Motley, "he began calmly to rely upon God's Providence in all the emergencies of his eventful life." [59]

The Calvinistic conscience was as much *Calvinistic* in evidence among the Dutch as among the *morality.* English Puritans. Says an Italian contemporary, "They hold adultery in horror." "They dispensed exact justice", says Campbell, "to poor and rich alike, cared for the unfortunate, and frowned on idleness and vice." "No one ever questioned their integrity. Public honesty is of later growth than that of individuals, men in a body often performing acts which singly they would condemn; but even here Holland has no superior in history. Throughout her long war with Spain, the national credit stood unimpaired. The towns, when

<hr>

[59] "Rise of Dutch Republic", vol. I. p. 699.

besieged, issued bonds which often were sold at a large discount, and men were found who, as in later times among ourselves, urged that the purchasers should only receive the money they had paid. No such counsels, however, prevailed in a single instance. The debts of the towns, like those of the State, were invariably paid in full." [60]

Results.

Of the results to civilization and humanity of that momentous conflict, which, in the strength of their creed, the Dutch Calvinists fought and won, we shall submit three brief summaries, each by an acknowledged master of historical learning.

Campbell's statement.

Says Campbell: "Out from this war of eighty years' duration emerged a republic, for two centuries the greatest in the world, a republic which was the instructor of the world in art, and whose corner-stone was religious toleration for all mankind." [61]

[60] "The Puritan in Holland, England and America", vol. I. pp. 87, 171.
[61] "Id., p. 133.

THE CREED TESTED BY ITS FRUITS

The above solid historical fact effectually *A theory ex-* disposes of the theory that Calvinism makes *ploded.* men haters of art or persecutors of their fellows. Whatever share Calvinists have had in the mistakes and superstitions of their age and race cannot be charged to their theological tenets. The Calvinistic zeal of the Dutch is beyond question, yet they burned no witches, they led the world in art, and before William Penn was born, taught and practiced the widest religious toleration. "In freedom of conscience", says Bancroft, "they were the light of the world." [62] The true father of modern religious liberty was the immortal Dutch Calvinist, William the Silent.

Motley's deliberate verdict is as follows: *Motley's* "Few strides more gigantic have been *verdict.* taken in the march of humanity than those by which a parcel of outlying provinces in the north of Europe exchanged slavery to a foreign despotism and to the Holy Inquisition for the position of a self-govern-

[62] "Hist. U. S.", vol. x. p. 58

ing commonwealth, in the front rank of contemporary powers, and in many respects the foremost of the world. It is impossible to calculate the amount of benefit rendered to civilization by the example of the Dutch Republic." [63]

Bancroft's estimate.

The following is Bancroft's estimate of what Calvinistic Holland has done for the world: "Of all the branches of the Germanic family that nation has endured the most and wrought the most in favor of liberty of conscience, liberty of commerce, and liberty in the State. For three generations the best interests of mankind were abandoned to its keeping; and to uphold the highest objects of spiritual life, its merchants, land holders, and traders so teemed with heroes and martyrs that they tired out brute force, and tyranny, and death itself, and from war educed life and hope for coming ages." [64]

Another demonstration.

Here, then, from history, we have an-

[63] "The United Netherlands", vol. IV. p. 549
[64] "Hist. U. S.", vol. x. p. 58.

other demonstration of the unequalled energizing and ennobling power of Calvinism. Above all the other doctrinal systems known to man, history crowns Calvinism as the creed of saints and heroes. To its Divine vitality and fruitfulness the modern world owes a debt of gratitude, which slowly in recent years it is beginning to recognize, but can never pay.

IN FRANCE.

In France the Calvinists were called *The Huguenots.* Huguenots. The character of the Huguenots the world knows. Their moral purity and heroism, whether persecuted at home or exiled abroad, has been the wonder of both friend and foe. " Their history ", says the Encyclopædia Britannica,[65] " is a standing marvel, illustrating the abiding power of strong religious convictions ". " The account of their endurance ", it declares, " is amongst the most remarkable and heroic records of religious history." According-

[65] Art. " Huguenots.''

ing to the great historian Lecky, himself a cold-blooded rationalist, the Huguenots were " the most solid, the most modest, the most virtuous, the most generally enlightened element in the French nation." [66]

The furious persecution that raged against them, of which the massacre of St. Bartholomew was a part and a sample, destroyed or exiled hundreds of thousands of Huguenots. The loss to France was irreparable. " It prepared the way ", says Lecky, " for the inevitable degradation of the national character and removed the last serious bulwark that might have broken the force of that torrent of skepticism and vice, which, a century later, laid prostrate in merited ruin, both the altar and the throne."

"Looking back", says an able writer, "at their sufferings, at the purity, self-denial, honesty, and industry of their lives, and at the devotion with which they adhered to religious duty and the worship of God, we

[66] " Eng. Hist. Eighteenth Century ", vol. 1. pp. 264, 265.

cannot fail to regard them as amongst the truest, greatest, and worthiest heroes of their age. In France they were the only men who were willing to die rather than forsake the worship of God according to the Scriptures and conscience." [67]

"Honest as Huguenot' To be "honest as a Huguenot" became a proverb, signalizing the highest reach of integrity. This quality, which is essential in the merchant who deals with foreigners whom he never sees, so characterized the business transactions of the Huguenots that the foreign trade of the country fell almost entirely into their hands.[68]

Eloquent silence. The eminent English writer, Samuel Smiles, known to thousands of Americans as the author of "Self Help", states that while the Huguenots were stigmatized in the contemporary literature of their enemies as "heretics", "atheists", "blasphemers", "monsters vomited forth of hell", not one word is to be found in these writ-

[67] "Calvinism in History", p. 122.
[68] Smiles' "The Huguenots", p. 134.

ings in impeachment of their morality and integrity. "The silence of their enemies on this point", says Smiles, "is perhaps the most eloquent testimony in their favor." [69]

The tree known by its fruits.

In a foot-note, Smiles makes a comment which is of especial interest coming from a man so distinguished for accuracy and sound judgment, and who, so far as we can learn, was committed in no way to the cause of Calvinism. "What the Puritan was in England", he says, " and the Covenanter in Scotland, that the Huguenot was in France; and that the system of Calvin should have developed precisely the same kind of men in these three several countries affords a remarkable illustration of the power of religious training in the formation of character." [70] Puritans, Huguenots, Covenanters! What a record and roll-call! What other creed in Christendom can show such a marvellous fruitage of purity

[69] Smiles' "The Huguenots", p. 134.
[70] Id., p. 134, note.

and heroism as these historic names represent?

What made the Huguenots to differ from
the rest of French Christendom? They
were of the same country, the same race,
the same natural traits and peculiarities,
oftentimes of the same household. What
made the difference? Let history answer:
" the system of Calvin ".

Near the middle of the seventeenth cen- *Jansen's*
tury a Roman Catholic Bishop and teacher *Augustine*
of theology, named Jansen, published an
exposition of the works of St. Augustine,
the greatest of the Church fathers. Augustine's doctrines of sin, sovereignty, predestination, and free grace, were the same
as those taught eleven centuries later by
Calvin, and four centuries earlier, as we believe, by Paul. To quote a common saying, Paul begat Augustine, and Augustine
begat Calvin.

Jansen's book was prohibited by a decree
of the Inquisition, and condemned as heret-

The Port Royal Calvinists. ical by the Pope. But it found its way into many hands. Especially at Port Royal, a Roman Catholic community and religious retreat not far from Paris, it was ardently studied and its doctrines warmly embraced. Immediately Port Royal became a theological storm-centre, the object of Jesuit hate and intrigue. After years of vicissitude and trial it was at last suppressed by the Papal power, but not till Calvinism had borne its characteristic fruit, and made Port Royal the synonym to succeeding ages of purity and intelligence.

Renan's testimony. Ernest Renan, the well-known author, scholar, scientist, and Member of the French Academy, was himself a rationalist, yet he calls St. Cyran, the Jansenist leader of the Port Royal school of thought, " the Calvin who took in hand the cause of God, to restore the faith of St. Paul and Augustine ". " This school ", he says, " was unequalled in the greatness of the characters it formed. Nowhere else have been seen so many brave and loyal spirits devoted absolutely to their ideal of righteousness. Port Royal rises in the midst of the seventeenth century like a triumphal column, a temple to manliness and truth." [71]

IN NEW ENGLAND.

The sterling character and worth of the Calvinists who settled New England has become a proverb. Puritans they were in fact as well as name. They reared their children to fear God, obey their parents, speak the truth, and practice industry and temperance. "One might dwell there from year to year", said a contemporary writer, " and not see a drunkard, or hear ar oath, or meet a beggar ". The consequence was universal health. The average duration of life in New England as compared with Europe was doubled. Of all who were born into the world more than two in ten, full four in nineteen, attained the age of seventy. Of those who lived beyond ninety the proportion as compared

The New England Puritans

[71] " Studies in Religious History and Criticism" pp. 424, 425.

with European tables of longevity was still more remarkable.[72]

Their religion was their life. It governed all their thoughts and relations. Beasts as well as men felt its influence. Cruelty to animals was a civil offense. In the humanity of their criminal laws they were two centuries ahead of their times.[73] In all their records Bancroft could find no example of divorce, an evidence of that Calvinistic conscience which, as Taine has told us, "enthroned purity on the domestic hearth".

Failings vs. virtues.

The mistakes and failings which they shared in common with their age are as nothing in comparison with their virtues. "Their transient persecutions in America", says Bancroft, "were in self-defense, and were no more than a train of mists hovering of an autumn morning over the channel of a fine river that diffused freshness and fertility wherever it wound." [74]

The Puritans of New England are a char-

[72] " Hist. U. S.", vol. I. p. 467.
[73] Id., p. 465.
[74] Id., p. 464.

acteristic example of the Calvinistic spirit *Calvinism* of intelligence and free inquiry. " Of all *and free inquiry.* contemporary sects ", says Bancroft, " they were the most free from credulity." [75]   The Pilgrim Fathers he pronounces " Calvinists in their faith according to the straitest system ", and says of them, " they renounced all attachment to human authority and reserved an entire and perpetual liberty of forming their principles and practice from the light that inquiry might shed upon their minds."[76] In this they but obeyed the impulse of their creed and the example of their spiritual father, Calvin, whom the same author describes as " pushing free inquiry to its utmost verge, and yet valuing inquiry solely as the means of arriving at fixed conclusions." [77]   It was in Calvinistic Holland, according to Smiles, that freedom of inquiry found its chief European centre.[78]

[75] " Hist. U. S.", vol. I. p. 463.
[76] Id., p. 300.
[77] " Miscellanies ", p. 407.
[78] " The Huguenots ", p. 177.

Intellectual superiority.

In his famous and profound work on the " History of Civilization ", Buckle, himself the adherent of no religious creed, remarks upon " the inquisitive spirit which has always accompanied Calvinism." [79] " The professors of Calvinism ", he says, " are more likely to acquire habits of independent thinking than those of Arminianism." [80] This would seem a safe inference from an admitted historical fact which Buckle thus states: " The most profound thinkers have been on the Calvinistic side; and it is interesting to observe that this superiority of thought on the part of the Calvinists existed from the beginning." [81] We quote in this connection the acknowledgment of an able and distinguished leader of American Methodism. Says Dr. Curry: " We concede to the Calvinistic churches the honor of having all along directed the best thinking of the country."

[79] Vol. i. p. 614.
[80] Id., p. 613.
[81] Id., p. 613, note.

This historic and habitual superiority *How ex-*
of Calvinists in the realm of intellect is no *plained.*
accident. It is the fruit of their creed.
Even Ralph Waldo Emerson admits and
admires the " mental concentration and
force " inspired by Calvinism, and lauds the
effect upon " character and intellect " of its
" determination of thought on the eternal
world ". Calvinism possesses the mind with
themes the most vital and majestic, " which
soar into the immeasurable blue and open
to thought celestial gates ". It gives foundation, consecration, inspiration to human
thought by its sublime doctrine of the
unity, stability, and order of all things in
God. The history of things heavenly and
earthly, spiritual and material, past, present, and to come, is a great whole in which
the Divine Will fulfils itself in its wisdom,
power, and goodness, all things coming
from God and returning to Him in the majesty of an imperial plan, formed before the
foundation of the world, whose unfolding
is Universal Providence, and whose goal

and consummation is that

"One far-off divine event
To which the whole creation moves."

Most satisfy-ing and stimulating. In this great and ennobling conception which takes us behind all that is phenomenal and bids us look at the eternities before and after our little day, every problem in theology, science, and philosophy finds its appropriate place, and to man's thinking faculty presents its inspiring challenge. Intellectually, Calvinism is at once the most satisfying and the most stimulating of creeds. It grapples with every difficulty. "It goes to the very root", says Morley, "of man's relations with the scheme of universal things." [82] Matthew Arnold, England's most acute and cultured critic of life and literature, has truly said that while "Arminianism, in the practical man's fashion, is apt to scrape the surface of things only", the Calvinist's "seriousness, force, and fervency" are begotten of

[82] "Oliver Cromwell", December *Century*, 1899.

THE CREED TESTED BY ITS FRUITS

"Calvinism's perpetual conversance with deep things and with the Bible."[83]   The believer in the Calvinistic system is no child playing with sandheaps on the seashore. He walks among hills and mountains.   The themes of thought around him tower upward, Alps on Alps.   His mental stature rises with his surroundings.   He becomes a thoughtful being, communing with sublimities.

To its characteristic elevation of thought *"Lofty* and life, writers of all shades of theological opinion bear unconscious witness in their use of the word "lofty" or its equivalent in connection with Calvinism.   Numberless illustrations might be given.   One of the latest is Theodore Roosevelt, in whose recent "Life of Cromwell" even the cursory reader must have noticed the recurrence of such expressions as "lofty creed", "lofty Presbyterianism", "lofty souls", "loftiness of aim", and the like, descriptive of the Calvinistic faith and spirit.

[83] "St. Paul and Protestantism", pp. 21, 26.

THE CREED TESTED BY ITS FRUITS.

Intelligence and education.

The elevation of the entire man sought and wrought by Calvinism is both cause and effect of the stress it has ever laid upon intelligence and education. Holding that man's chief end is to glorify God, it seeks the development and training of the whole manhood, intellectual as well as spiritual, as faculty for the attainment of this divinely appointed end. It is natural, therefore, that Calvinism's greatest expounder should have been also the greatest educational benefactor of the modern world. " We boast ", says Bancroft, " of our common schools; Calvin was the father of popular education, the inventor of the system of free schools." [84] " Wherever Calvinism gained dominion ", he says again, " it invoked intelligence for the people and in every parish planted the common school." [85]

> " It dreads no skeptic's puny hands,
> While near the school the church-spire stands;
> Nor fears the blinded bigot's rule
> While near the church-spire stands the school."

[84] " Miscellanies ", p. 406.
[85] " Hist. U. S.", vol. II. p. 463.

To the heroic survivors of the memorable siege of Leyden, William the Silent offered as a reward of their patriotism a reduction of taxes or the establishment of a school of learning. They chose the latter. That was the origin of the University of Leyden, renowned throughout the whole world, whose three-hundredth anniversary twenty-five years ago was celebrated with befitting solemnities. It stands a monument of that Calvinistic love of learning which, putting mind above money, has inspired countless generations of God-fearing Calvinists to pinch themselves to the bone to educate their children. "That any being with capacity for knowledge should die ignorant, this I call a tragedy." In this thrilling dictum of Carlyle, giving the word knowledge its highest reach and noblest purpose, throbs the heart of Calvinism. *The heart of Calvinism.*

IN SCOTLAND.

The best possible place to study the effects of a particular system of religion is a

The best studying ground. country in which for generations that system has had full sway and a free hand. To know the practical fruits of Roman Catholicism we should examine some country like Spain or Brazil, where for centuries Romanism has been the one religion, unhelped and unhindered by other systems. There is one land in which Calvinism has long been practically the one religion. That land is Scotland.

The Scotch before Calvinism. When Calvinism reached the Scotch people, they were vassals of the Romish church, priest-ridden, ignorant, wretched, degraded in body, mind, and morals. Buckle describes them as "filthy in their persons and in their homes", "poor and miserable", "excessively ignorant and excessively superstitious", "with superstition engrained into their characters." [86]

"The last shall be first." Marvellous was the transformation when the great doctrines learned by Knox from the Bible in Scotland and more thoroughly at Geneva while sitting at the feet

[86] "Hist. of Civilization", vol. II. pp. 140, 145. 153.

98

of Calvin, flashed in upon their minds. It was like the sun rising at midnight. Says Carlyle: "This that Knox did for his nation we may really call a resurrection as from death." "John Knox", says Froude, "was the one man without whom Scotland as the modern world has known it, would have had no existence."[87] Knox made Calvinism the religion of Scotland, and Calvinism made Scotland the moral standard for the world. It is certainly a significant fact that in that country where there is the most of Calvinism there should be the least of crime; that of all the peoples of the world to-day that nation which is confessedly the most moral is also the most thoroughly Calvinistic; that in that land where Calvinism has had supremest sway individual and national morality has reached its loftiest level.

Henry M. Stanley, the famous explorer, *Stanley's* is one of the shrewdest judges of men that *testimony* this generation has produced. His insight

[87] "Hist. Eng.", vol. x. p. 454.

into character and acuteness of observation were the means again and again of saving his own life and that of his men amid the wilds of heathenism. His travels have brought him into close personal contact with missionaries of every church and nationality. Though no Scotchman himself, Stanley pronounces Scotch missionaries the best and most successful in the world; and their superiority he attributes to that supreme devotion to duty taught them in their Calvinistic homes.[88]

"Spiritual conquerors of the world." Stanley's testimony to the pre-eminent power and success of the missionaries trained by Calvinism reminds us of a similar tribute by the great historian D'Aubigné. "Luther", he says, "transformed princes into heroes of the faith; the reformation of Calvin was addressed particularly to the people, among whom it raised up martyrs until the time came when

[88] For an exquisite and inspiring picture, drawn from life, of a Scotch Calvinistic home, see appendix to this chapter.

it was to send forth the spiritual conquerors of the world. For three centuries it has been producing in the social condition of the nations that have received it, transformations unknown to former times. And still at this very day, and now perhaps more than ever, it imparts to the men who accept it a spirit of power which makes them chosen instruments fitted to propagate truth, morality, and civilization to the ends of the earth." [89]

Another significant fact. Scotland leads *Intellectual* the world not only in the average morality, *pre-eminence.* but also in the average intelligence of its people. This was to have been expected. Calvinism, as we have seen, elevates the whole man. The study of its comprehensive and logical system of doctrine is itself an unsurpassed mental discipline and stimulus. "The effect of familiarity with the Shorter Catechism upon the intellectual character of the Scottish peasantry", says

[89] "Reformation in the Time of Calvin", vol. I., preface, p. x.

Morley, "is one of the accepted common-places of history." [90]   "In every branch of knowledge", says Buckle, "this once poor and ignorant people produced original and successful thinkers.   What makes this the more remarkable is its complete contrast to their former state." [91]   Says Prof. Fiske: "One need not fear contradiction in saying that no other people in modern times, in proportion to their numbers, have achieved so much in all departments of human activity as the people of Scotland have achieved.   It would be superfluous to mention the pre-eminence of Scotland in the industrial arts, or to recount the glorious names in philosophy, in history, in poetry and romance, and in every department of science which have made Scotland illustrious for all future time." [92]   Prof. Fiske proceeds to remark upon the patent fact that

[90] "Oliver Cromwell", *Century Magazine*, February, 1900.
[91] "Hist. of Civilization", vol. II. p. 253.
[92] "Beginnings of New England", p. 152.

"this magnificent intellectual fruition" is the outcome of "Calvinistic orthodoxy."

Here then is a matter of profound sig- *Summation* nificance, that that land whose previous degradation was notorious, and which for three centuries has been of all lands the most intensely and exclusively Calvinistic, to-day surpasses every other nation on the globe in both the intellectual and the moral glory of its people.

America has never produced a man of *Lowell's* wider information, or more varied and brill- *testimony.* iant gifts, than James Russell Lowell, the renowned diplomat, essayist, and poet. Lowell's connection from childhood was with a religious body not Calvinistic; yet he says: "If the Calvinistic churches are to be judged by the results of their teaching upon character and conduct, as seen in Scotland and New England, then these churches are entitled to the highest praise. For the superiority is not solely in morality and intelligence, but in the prevalent sense of duty, in high ideals and inflexible principles, and, in short, in the consciousness of the spiritual world that is an eternal *now* with believers. After due allowance made for time-servers and hypocrites, I think there are among the Calvinists more godly men, each living ' As ever in his great Taskmaster's eye ', than in any other branch of the Christian Church." [93]

Review and conclusion. We have not space to pursue this branch of our subject further, though we have but dipped into it here and there. We have endeavored to try Calvinism by Christ's own test of fruitfulness, of practical results. We have examined its workings in many countries and amid conditions the most diverse and adverse. We have conducted the investigation under the guidance, not of Calvinistic partisans, but of authors and observers of worldwide reputation for ability and learning, whose prepossessions in almost every case would naturally be rather against than for Calvin-

[93] Quoted by the *Reformed Church Messenger*, 1896, from a published sketch of Lowell.

ism. The conclusion to which they lead us represents the impartial verdict of history. That conclusion is, that as a character builder, as a purifying, energizing, uplifting force in the life of men and nations, Calvinism stands supreme among the religious systems of the world. And further, since truth is in order to godliness, and the tree is to be judged by its fruit, we have here the historical demonstration that the Calvinistic is the truest creed of Christendom.

This tree, to adapt another's eloquent *The old oak.* paragraph,[94] may have, to prejudiced eyes, a rough bark, a gnarled stem, and boughs twisted often into knotted shapes of ungraceful strength. But, remember, it is not a willow-wand of yesterday. These boughs have wrestled with the storms of a thousand years; this stem has been wreathed with the red lightning and scarred by the thunderbolt; and all over its rough rind are the marks of the battle-axe

[94] Dr. T. V. Moore's "Power and Claims of a Calvinistic Literature", p. 35.

and the bullet. This old oak has not the pliant grace and silky softness of a green-house plant, but it has a majesty above grace, and a grandeur beyond beauty. Its roots may be strangely contorted, but some of them are rich with the blood of glorious battle-fields, some of them are clasped around the stakes of martyrs; some of them hidden in solitary cells and lonely libraries, where deep thinkers have mused and prayed, as in some apocalyptic Patmos; and its great tap-root runs back, until it twines in living and loving embrace around the cross of Calvary. Its boughs may be gnarled, but they hang clad with all that is richest and strongest in the civilization and Christianity of human history.

APPENDIX.

A Scotch Presbyterian Home.

We have never heard or read a sermon on family religion which impressed us more deeply than the following simple narra-tive of the religious home-life of an humble

Scotch family. It is taken from the first chapter of the Autobiography of John G. Paton, missionary to the New Hebrides:

"And so began in his early life that blessed custom of Family Prayer, morning and evening, which my father practised probably without one single omission till he lay on his deathbed, seventy-seven years of age; when, even to the last day of his life, a portion of Scripture was read, and his voice was heard softly joining in the Psalm, and his lips breathed the morning and evening Prayer, falling in sweet benediction on the heads of all his children, far away many of them over all the earth, but all meeting him there at the Throne of Grace. None of us can remember that any day ever passed unhallowed thus; no hurry for market, no rush to business, no arrival of friends or guests, no trouble or sorrow, no joy or excitement, ever prevented at least our kneeling around the family altar, while the high priest led our prayers to God, and offered himself and his children there.

"And blessed to others, as well as to ourselves, was the light of such example! I have heard that, in long after years, the worst woman in the village of Torthorwald, then leading an immoral life, but since changed by the grace of God, was known to declare, that the only thing that kept her from despair and from the hell of the suicide was when in the dark winter nights she crept close up underneath my father's window, and heard him pleading in family worship that God would convert ' the sinner from the error of wicked ways and polish him as a jewel for the Redeemer's crown.' ' I felt ', said she, ' that I was a burden on that good man's heart, and I knew that God would not disappoint him. That thought kept me out of hell, and at last led me to the only Saviour.'

"Each of us, from very early days, considered it no penalty, but a great joy, to go with our father to the church; the four miles were a treat to our young spirits, the company by the way was a fresh incitement, and occasionally some of the wonders of city life rewarded our eager eyes. A few other pious men and women of the best evangelical type went from the same parish to one or other favourite minister at Dumfries,—and when these God-fearing peasants 'forgathered' in the way to or from the house of God, we youngsters had sometimes rare glimpses of what Christian talk may be and ought to be. They went to the church, full of beautiful expectancy of spirit—their souls were on the outlook for God; they returned from the church, ready and even anxious to exchange ideas as to what they had heard and received of the things of life. I have to bear my testimony that religion was presented to us with a great deal of intellectual freshness, and that it did not repel us but kindled our spiritual interest. The talks which we heard were, however, genuine; not the make-believe of religious conversation, but the sincere outcome of their own personalities. That, perhaps, makes all the difference betwixt talk that attracts and talk that drives away.

" We had, too, special Bible Readings on the Lord's Day evening,—mother and children and visitors reading in turns, with fresh and interesting question, answer and exposition, all tending to impress us with the infinite grace of a God of love and mercy in the great gift of His dear Son Jesus, our Saviour. The Shorter Catechism was gone through regularly, each answering the question asked, till the whole had been explained, and its foundation in Scripture shown by the proof-texts adduced. It has been an amazing thing to me, occasionally to meet with men who blamed this ' catechizing ' for giving them a distaste to religion; every one in all our circle thinks and feels exactly the opposite. It laid the solid rock-foundation of our religious life. After-years have given to these questions and their answers a deeper or a modified meaning, but none of us have ever once even dreamed of wishing that we had been otherwise trained. Of course, if the parents are not devout, sincere, and affectionate,—if the whole affair on both sides is taskwork, or worse, hypocritical and false, —results must be very different indeed!

"Oh, I can remember those happy Sabbath evenings; no blinds drawn, and shutters up, to keep out the sun from us, as some scandalously affirm; but a holy, happy, entirely human day, for a Christian father, mother, and children to spend. How my father would parade across and across our flag-floor, telling over the substance of the day's sermons to our dear mother, who, because of the great distance and because of her many living 'encumbrances', got very seldom indeed to the church, but gladly embraced every chance, when there was prospect or promise of a 'lift' either way from some friendly gig! How he would entice us to help him to recall some idea or other, rewarding us when we got the length of 'taking notes' and reading them over on our return; how he would turn the talk ever

so naturally to some Bible story, or some
martyr reminiscence, or some happy allu-
sion to the ' Pilgrim's Progress'! And then
it was quite a contest, which of us would
get reading aloud, while all the rest list-
ened, and father added here and there a
happy thought, or illustration, or anecdote.

"Others must write and say what they will,
and as they feel; but so must I. There were
eleven of us brought up in a home like that;
and never one of the eleven, boy or girl,
man or woman, has been heard, or ever will
be heard, saying that Sabbath was dull or
wearisome for us, or suggesting that we
have heard of or seen any way more likely
than that for making the day of the Lord
bright and blessed alike for parents and for
children. But God help the homes where
these things are done by force and not by
love! The very discipline through which
our father passed us was a kind of religion
in itself. If anything really serious required
to be punished, he retired first to his closet
for prayer, and we boys got to understand

that he was laying the whole matter before God; and that was the severest part of the punishment for me to bear. I could have defied any amount of mere penalty, but this spoke to my conscience as a message from God. We loved him all the more, when we saw how much it cost him to punish us; and, in truth, he had never very much of that kind of work to do upon any one of all the eleven—we were ruled by love far more than by fear.

"Our home consisted of a 'but' and a 'ben' and a 'mid-room', or chamber, called the 'closet'. The one end was my mother's domain, and served all the purposes of dining-room and kitchen and parlor, besides containing two large wooden erections, called by our Scotch peasantry 'box-beds'; not holes in the wall, as in cities, but grand, big, airy beds, adorned with many-coloured counterpanes, and hung with natty curtains, showing the skill of the mistress of the house. The other end was my father's workshop, filled with

five or six ' stocking frames ', whirring with
the constant action of five or six pairs of
busy hands and feet, and producing right
genuine hosiery for the merchants at
Hawick and Dumfries. The ' closet ' was a
very small apartment betwixt the other
two, having room only for a bed, a little
table, and a chair, with a diminutive window shedding diminutive light on the scene.
This was the Sanctuary of that cottage
home. Thither daily, and oftentimes a day,
generally after each meal, we saw our father retire, and ' shut to the door '; and we
children got to understand by a sort of
spiritual instinct (for the thing was too sacred to be talked about) that prayers were
being poured out there for us, as of old by
the High Priest within the veil in the Most
Holy Place. We occasionally heard the pa-
thetic echoes of a trembling voice pleading
as if for life, and we learned to slip out and
in past that door on tiptoe, not to disturb
the holy colloquy. The outside world
might not know, but we knew, whence

came that happy light as of a new-born smile that always was dawning on my father's face: it was a reflection from the Divine Presence, in the consciousness of which he lived. Never, in temple or cathedral, on mountain or in glen, can I hope to feel that the Lord God is more near, more visibly walking and talking with men, than under that humble cottage roof of thatch and oaken wattles. Though everything else in religion were by some unthinkable catastrophe to be swept out of memory, or blotted from my understanding, my soul would wander back to those early scenes, and shut itself up once again in that Sanctuary closet, and, hearing still the echoes of those cries to God, would hurl back all doubt with the victorious appeal, ' He walked with God, why may not I?'

" His happy partner, 'Wee Jen', died in 1865, and he himself in 1868, having reached his seventy-seventh year,—an altogether beautiful and noble episode of human existence having been enacted, amid the humblest surroundings of a Scottish peasant's home, through the influence of their united love by the grace of God; and in this world, or in any world, all their children will rise up at mention of their names and call them blessed."

III

THE CREED TESTED BY ITS FRUITS
(CONTINUED)

" Ye shall know the truth, and the truth shall make you free."—John 8 : 32.

III

THE CREED TESTED BY ITS FRUITS (*Continued*)

AMERICA'S DEBT TO CALVINISM.

If the average American citizen were *The founder* asked, who was the founder of America, *of America.* the true author of our giant Republic, he might be puzzled to answer. We can imagine his amazement at hearing the answer given to this question by the famous German historian, Ranke, one of the profoundest scholars of modern times. Says Ranke, "John Calvin was the virtual founder of America."

If this be true, every American should know it. Let us see.

At the time of the Revolution the estimated population of our country was

THE CREED TESTED BY ITS FRUITS

*Early mate-
rial of our
Republic.*

3,000,000. Of this number 900,000 were of
Scotch or Scotch-Irish origin, 600,000 were
Puritan English, while over 400,000 were
of Dutch, German Reformed, and Huguenot descent.[1] That is to say, two thirds of
our Revolutionary forefathers were trained
in the school of Calvin. Since these two
thirds included the New England colonists
and the Scotch-Irish immigrants, pronounced by the learned author of " American Christianity " " the two most master-
ful races on the continent ",[2] " the two
streams ", as Dr. F. W. Gunsaulus says,
" apparently most effective and important
in the creation of great things, intellectual
and spiritual, in our American life ",[3] their
preponderance in influence was even more
marked than in numbers.

[1] W. H. Roberts, " Proceedings Seventh General
Council, 1899 ", p. 94.

[2] " Hist. of American Christianity ", by Leonard
Woolsey Bacon (1900), p. 292.

[3] *The American Monthly Review of Reviews*, February,
1901, p. 167.

Where learned they those immortal prin- *Calvinism* ciples of the rights of man, of human lib- *and human* erty, equality, and self-government, on *rights.* which they based our Republic, and which form to-day the distinctive glory of our American civilization? In the school of Calvin they learned them. There the modern world learned them. So history teaches.

Says Bancroft: " Calvinism was revolu- *A democratic* tionary; it taught as a Divine revelation the *religion.* natural equality of man." " It is the essential tendency of Calvinism ", says Doyle, the eminent Oxford scholar, " to destroy all distinctions of rank, and all claims to superiority which rest on wealth or political expediency." [4] " Calvinism is essentially democratic ",[5] says Buckle in his History of Civilization. " A democratic and republican religion ",[6] it is called by De Tocqueville, one of the ablest political

[4] " The English in America ", by J. A. Doyle, M.A., p. 9.

[5] " Hist. of Civilization ", vol I. p. 669.

[6] " Democracy ", vol. I. p. 384.

writers of the century. "Calvinism opposed", says Bancroft, "hereditary monarchy, aristocracy, and bondage."[7] John Richard Green, the author of the greatest history of the English people yet written, belonged to the Anglican church. Yet he says: "It is in Calvinism that the modern world strikes its roots; for it was Calvinism that first revealed the worth and dignity of man. Called of God, and heir of heaven, the trader at his counter and the digger in his field suddenly rose into equality with the noble and the king."[8] "In that mighty elevation of the masses", he says again, "which was embodied in the Calvinist doctrines of election and grace, lay the germs of the modern principles of human equality."

Effect of Calvinistic teaching illustrated. "The fruits of such a teaching", continues Green, "soon showed themselves in a new attitude of the people. 'Here', said Melville, over the grave of John Knox,

[7] "Hist. U. S.", vol. II. p. 464.
[8] "Hist. of Eng. People", vol. III. p. 114.

' here lies one who never feared the face of man '; and if Scotland still reverences the memory of the reformer, it is because at that grave her peasant and her trader learned to look in the face of nobles and kings and ' not be ashamed '." [9] To the effect of these " doctrines of election and grace " taught by Knox, Froude also testifies, saying: " His was the voice which taught the peasant of the Lothians that he was a free man, the equal in the sight of God with the proudest peer or prelate that had trampled on his forefathers. He it was that raised the poor Commons of his country . . . into men whom neither king, noble, nor priest could force again to submit to tyranny." [10]

The learned author of " The United States as a Nation " makes the following eloquent acknowledgment of the relation of the Calvinistic theology to liberty: It "inspires a resolute, almost defiant, freedom

" Such faith is freedom."

[9] " Hist. of Eng. People ", vol. III. p. 446.
[10] " Hist. Eng.", vol. x. p. 457.

in those who deem themselves the subjects
of God's electing grace: in all things they
are more than conquerors through the confidence that nothing shall be able to separate them from the love of God. No
doctrine of the dignity of human nature, of
the rights of man, of national liberty, of
social equality, can create such a resolve
for the freedom of the soul as this personal
conviction of God's favoring and protect-
ing sovereignty. He who has this faith
feels he is compassed about with everlasting love, guided with everlasting strength;
his will is the tempered steel that no fire
can melt, no force can break. Such faith is
freedom; and this spiritual freedom is the
source and strength of all other freedom." [11]

Prof. Fiske of Harvard, himself not ecclesiastically allied in any way with Calvinism, affirms that "The promulgation of
Calvin's theology was one of the longest
steps that mankind have taken toward per-

[11] p. 30, quoted by McFetridge.

sonal freedom." "It was a religion", he says, "fit to inspire men who were to be called upon to fight for freedom." [12]

"Calvinism", says Froude, "has inspired and maintained the bravest efforts ever made to break the yoke of unjust authority." [13]

Before proving its power in the new *Previous* world, Calvinism had fought and won the *achievements.* fight for freedom in the old. Not only in Scotland, as we have seen, but also in England and Holland it had challenged and conquered tyranny. To the Puritans, declares Hume, a hater of Calvinism, England owes "the whole freedom of her constitution." [14] Says Motley, not ecclesiastically committed himself to Calvinism: "The battle that saved England to constitutional liberty was fought and won by Calvinists." Of Holland the same eminent historian says: "The Reformation had

[12] "The Beginnings of New England", pp. 58, 59.
[13] "Short Studies on Great Subjects", p. 13.
[14] "Hist. Eng.", vol. v. p. 134.

entered the Netherlands by the Walloon (Calvinistic) gate. The earliest and most eloquent preachers, the most impassioned converts, the sublimest martyrs, had lived, preached, fought, suffered, and died with the precepts of Calvin in their heart. The fire which had consumed the last vestige of royal and sacerdotal despotism throughout the independent republic had been lighted by the hands of Calvinists." [15]

The makers, therefore, of free Holland, free England, free Scotland, were earlier pupils in the same school that moulded the makers of free America.

Church government. As might have been expected, Calvinism's revolutionary principles of liberty and equality found expression in a system of church government equally revolutionary. The people of Christ, it taught, were to be governed and ministered to, not by the appointees of any one man or set of men placed over them, but by pastors and officers elected by themselves.

[15] " The United Netherlands ", vol. III. p. 120.

THE CREED TESTED BY ITS FRUITS

With the principle and right of self-gov- *Revolution-ary republic-anism.* ernment embodied in this plan, we, in America at least, are now happily familiar. Three and a half centuries ago it was so novel and revolutionary as to shake the whole civil, social, and religious world to its centre.

> " For all the past of time reveals
> A bridal dawn of thunder-peals,
> Wherever Thought hath wedded Fact."

" The right exercised by each congregation of electing its own ministers was in itself ", says Bancroft, " a moral revolution. Religion was now with the people, not over the people." [16] Sir James Stephen, the eminent English statesman and jurist, for ten years Professor of Modern History in the University of Cambridge, a member himself of the Anglican Church, in speaking of the ecclesiastical organization effected by the General Synod of France,

[16] " Hist. U. S.", vol I. p. 462.

which met May 25th, 1559, says: " A great
social revolution had thus been effected.
Within the centre of the French monarchy,
Calvin and his disciples had established a
spiritual republic, and had solemnly recognized as the basis of it four principles—
each germinant of results of the highest importance to the political commonwealth.
These principles were, first, that the will of
the people was the one legitimate source of
the power of their rulers; secondly, that
power was most properly delegated by the
people to their rulers, by means of elec-
tions, in which every adult man might exercise the right of suffrage; thirdly, that in
ecclesiastical government, the clergy and
laity were entitled to an equal and co-ordi-
nate authority; and, fourthly, that between
the Church and State, no alliance, or mutual dependence, or other definite relation,
necessarily or properly existed." [17] Calvin's church organization Green calls " a
Christian republic ", " a Christian state in

[17] " Lectures on the Hist. of France ", p. 415.

which the true sovereign was not Pope or Bishop but the Christian man." [18]

By its coronation of the individual man as sovereign, Calvin's organization clashed not only with the rule of Pope and Bishop, but with all those despotic and aristocratic ideas and customs which had dominated and darkened the world for ages.

Birth of the modern world.

> " And Freedom reared in that august sunrise
>   Her beautiful bold brow."

" Presbytery agreeth as well with monarchy ", declared despotic King James, " as God and the devil." The Calvinistic system, " the monarchs of that day ", says Bancroft, " with one consent and with instinctive judgment feared as republicanism." [19] " As a vast and consecrated democracy ", says Green, " it stood in contrast with the whole social and political framework of the European nations." [20] It

[18] "Hist. Eng. People ", vol. III. p. 113.
[19] "Hist. U. S.", vol. II. p. 461.
[20] "Hist. Eng. People ", vol. III. p. 114.

marked the opening of a new chapter in the history of humanity.

Benefactor of mankind.

Had Calvin done nothing more than to make government of the people, by the people, for the people, a startling and triumphant reality in the earth, he would have deserved well of mankind. Says Bancroft, " More truly benevolent to the human race than Solon, more self-denying than Lycurgus, the genius of Calvin infused enduring elements into the institutions of Geneva and made it for the modern world the impregnable fortress of popular liberty, the fertile seedplot of democracy." [21]

Calvin's home.

The city of Geneva, in Switzerland, on the shores of Lake Geneva, called also Lake Leman, was the home of Calvin. Here he had his church, which Knox, who came to Geneva, like ten thousand other Bible students from all parts of Europe, to sit an admiring pupil at Calvin's feet, pronounced " the most perfect school of Christ

[21] " Miscellanies ", p. 406.

that ever was since the days of the Apostles."

From Geneva his influence radiated into *Influence* every corner of Christendom. "Calvin's true home", as Schaff says, "was the Church of God. He broke through all national limitations. There was scarcely a monarch or statesman or scholar of his age with whom he did not come in contact. Every people of Europe was represented among his disciples. He helped to shape the religious character of churches and nations yet unborn. The Huguenots of France, the Protestants of Holland and Belgium, the Puritans and Independents of England and New England, the Presbyterians of Scotland and throughout the world, yea, we may say, the whole Anglo-Saxon race, in its prevailing religious character and institutions, bear the impress of his genius, and show the power and tenacity of his doctrines and principles of government." [22]

[22] "Creeds of Christendom", vol. I. p. 444.

Calvinism and America. Those revolutionary principles of republican liberty and self-government, taught and embodied in the system of Calvin, were brought to America, and in this new land where they have borne so mighty a harvest were planted, by whose hands?—the hands of Calvinists. The vital relation of Calvin and Calvinism to the founding and free institutions of America, however strange in some ears the statement of Ranke may have sounded, is recognized and affirmed by historians of all lands and creeds.

D'Aubigné's testimony. Says D'Aubigné, whose " History of the Reformation " is a classic: " Calvin was the founder of the greatest of republics. The pilgrims who left their country in the reign of James I., and, landing on the barren soil of New England, founded populous and mighty colonies, were his sons, his direct and legitimate sons; and that American nation which we have seen growing so rapidly boasts as its father the humble Reformer on the shores of Lake Leman." [23]

[23] " Reformation in the Time of Calvin ", vol. I. p. 5.

The famous French critic and historian, *Taine's* Taine, holding no religious faith himself, *testimony* yet declares of the Calvinists: " These men are the true heroes of England. They founded England, in spite of the corruption of the Stuarts, by the exercise of duty, by the practice of justice, by obstinate toil, by vindication of right, by resistance to oppression, by the conquest of liberty, by the repression of vice. They founded Scotland; they founded the United States; at this day they are, by their descendants, founding Australia and colonizing the world." [24]

Says Motley: " In England the seeds of *Motley's* liberty, wrapped up in Calvinism and *testimony.* hoarded through many trying years, were at last destined to float over land and sea, and to bear largest harvests of temperate freedom for great commonwealths that were still unborn." [25]   " The Calvinists

[24] " English Literature ", vol. II. p. 472 (as quoted by McFetridge).
[25] " The United Netherlands ", vol. III. p. 121.

THE CREED TESTED BY ITS FRUITS

founded the commonwealths of England, of Holland, and of America." [26] " To Calvinists ", he says again, " more than to any other class of men, the political liberties of England, Holland, and America are due." [27]

Schaff's testimony

Says Philip Schaff, the Origen of the modern world: " The principles of the Republic of the United States can be traced thro' the intervening link of Puritanism to Calvinism, which, with all its theological rigor, has been the chief educator of manly characters and promoter of constitutional freedom in modern times." [28]

Choate's testimony

Says Rufus Choate, the great American lawyer, in his oration on " The Age of the Pilgrims, Our Heroic Period ": " In the reign of Mary, from 1553 to 1558, a thousand learned Englishmen fled from the stake at home to the happier states of continental Protestantism. Of these, great

[26] " The United Netherlands ", vol. IV. p. 548.
[27] Id., p. 547.
[28] " Creeds of Christendom ", p. 219.

134

numbers—I know not how many—came to Geneva. I ascribe to that five years in Geneva an influence which has changed the face of the world. I seem to myself to trace to it, as an influence on the English character, a new theology, new politics, another tone of character, the opening of another era of time and liberty. I seem to myself to trace to it the great civil war in England, the republican constitution framed in the cabin of the *Mayflower*, the theology of Jonathan Edwards, the battle of Bunker Hill, the Independence of America." [29]

The conclusions of the famous Spanish scholar, orator, and statesman, Emilio Castelar, at one time Professor of History in the University of Madrid, are of special interest and value. As a Roman Catholic, he hated Calvin and Calvinism. He says: " It was necessary for the republican movement of America that there should come a morality more austere than Luther's, the morality of Calvin, and a Church more dem-

Castelar's testimony.

[29] "Works of Rufus Choate", vol. I. p. 378.

ocratic than the German, the Church of Geneva. The Anglo-Saxon democracy has for its only lineage a book of a primitive society—the Bible. It is the product of a severe theology learned by the few Christian fugitives in the gloomy cities of Holland and of Switzerland, where the morose shade of Calvin still wanders. . . . And it remains serenely in its grandeur, forming the most dignified, most moral, most enlightened and richest portion of the human race." [30] One feels like asking Castelar how a fountain so bitter could send forth such sweet waters.

Bancroft's testimony.

Says Bancroft: "The light of Calvin's genius shattered the mask of darkness which Superstition had held for centuries before the brow of Religion. Calvinism inspired its converts to cross the Atlantic and sail away from the traditions of the Church, from hereditary power, from the sovereignty of earthly kings, and from all dominion but that of the Bible and such as

[30] *Harper's Monthly*, June and July, 1872.

136

arose from natural reason and equity. He that will not honor the memory and respect the influence of Calvin knows but little of the origin of American liberty." [31]

Not only did Calvinism imbue its converts with the spirit of liberty, it gave them practical training in the rights and duties of freemen. Each Calvinistic congregation having largely an independent life of its own, and conducting its own affairs through officers of its own election, constituted, as Fiske affirms, "one of the most effective schools that has ever existed for training men in local self-government." [32]

Invaluable training school.

The influence of the doctrines of Calvinism upon character we have seen in a former chapter. How powerfully also its method of church government, especially in its fully developed Presbyterian form, tends to foster in the individual that high and self-respecting type of manhood which alone gives success and permanence to free

Church government and character.

[31] "Miscellanies", pp. 406, 407.
[32] "The Beginnings of New England", p. 59.

institutions is matter of history and observation.

Illustration. For example, an English writer, of Episcopalian sympathies, Mr. Richard Heath, testifies to the excellent effect of the Presbyterian system where it has crossed the Scottish border and established itself in the northern shires of England: " The Northumbrian peasant is largely influenced by a form of Christianity that not only recognizes that he is a man, but that, without ceasing to be a laboring man, tending the sheep or following the plow, he can be chosen, and is chosen, and found worthy to be an elder of the church." He goes on to speak of " the superior educative power of the Presbyterian to the Church of England system, as seen in the higher form of manhood and womanhood of the people under its control. The reason is clear: the one is a democratic religion, the other the most aristocratic in the world." [33]

[33] " American Church History ", vol. VI. p. 293 (1900).

THE CREED TESTED BY ITS FRUITS

Should any member of a Presbyterian church feel that injustice has been done him by the Session, through misapprehension or through any local or personal prejudice, he can appeal, if he will, to the Presbytery, and thence, if he will, to the Synod, and thence, if he will, to the General Assembly. The rights of the youngest, poorest, humblest member are thus safeguarded to the uttermost. *Individual rights safeguarded.*

The well-nigh perfect manner in which justice, freedom, order, and all the ends of popular self-government are secured by the Presbyterian system of graded representative assemblies, with executive, legislative, and judicial functions, all distinct, yet all working together as component parts of a well-ordered whole, has won the admiration of thinking men of all creeds. Testimony from a remarkable source is that of the late able and distinguished Roman Catholic, Archbishop Hughes of New York: " Though it is my privilege ", he wrote, " to regard the authority exercised *" Without an equal or a rival."*

by the General Assembly as usurpation, still I must say, with every man acquainted with the mode in which it is organized, that for the purposes of popular and political government its structure is little inferior to that of Congress itself. It acts on the principle of a radiating centre, and is without an equal or a rival among the other denominations of the country." [34]

Amazing " coincidence."

The striking similarity between the constitution of the Presbyterian Church and that of the United States has excited much wondering comment. The Hon. W. C. Preston of South Carolina wrote: " Certainly it was the most remarkable and singular coincidence that the constitution of the Presbyterian Church should bear such a close and striking resemblance to the political constitution of our country." [35]

The explanation.

Upon this " most remarkable and singular coincidence " a few facts from history

[34] Quoted in " Presbyterians and the Revolution ", p. 28.

[35] " Scotch and Irish Seeds ", p 346.

may shed light. In Green's " History of
the English People " we read, the reader re-
membering that kirk is Scotch for church:
" The moral power which Knox created
was to express itself through the ecclesiastical forms which had been devised by the
genius of Calvin.[36] The new force of popular opinion was concentrated and formu-
lated in an ordered system of Kirk-Sessions
and Presbyteries and provincial Synods,
while chosen delegates formed the General
Assembly of the Kirk. In this organization of her churches Scotland saw herself
for the first time the possessor of a really
representative system, of a popular government. Not only did Presbyterianism bind
Scotland together, as it had never been
bound before, by its administrative organization, but it called the people at large to
a voice, and, as it turned out, a decisive
voice, in the administration of affairs. No

[36] More accurately, " which had been developed by
the genius of Calvin from the principles laid down in
Scripture."

141

church constitution has proved in practice
so democratic as that of Scotland. Its influence in raising the nation at large to a
consciousness of its power was shown by
the change which passed from the moment
of its establishment over the face of Scotch
history." [87]

The national model. That was two centuries before the
achievement of American independence.
When, therefore, the fathers of our Republic sat down to frame a system of representative popular government, their task was
not so difficult as some have imagined.
They had a model to work by. As Chief
Justice Tilghman says: "The framers of
the Constitution of the United States borrowed very much of the form of our Republic from the Constitution of the Presbyterian Church of Scotland."

Summary. We see then that Calvinism furnished
the foundation principles of our Republic;
it supplied the best and largest part of the
early material of our Republic; it served as

[87] " Hist. of Eng. People ", vol. III. p. 447.

THE CREED TESTED BY ITS FRUITS

the invaluable training school of our Republic; it furnished the model for the immortal constitution of our Republic. It remains to show the leading part that Calvinism took in securing the national independence that guaranteed the life of our Republic.

The briefest statement will here suffice. *"A Presbyterian measure."* The facts are undisputed. They are summed up in two sentences by Bancroft: "The Revolution of 1776, as far as it was affected by religion, was a Presbyterian measure. It was the natural outgrowth of the principles which the Presbyterianism of the Old World planted in her sons, the English Puritans, the Scotch Covenanters, the French Huguenots, the Dutch Calvinists, and the (Scotch-Irish) Presbyterians of Ulster."[38]

As late as August, 1775, Thomas Jefferson said: "I would rather be in dependence on Great Britain, properly limited, *The first voice in America.*

[38] Quoted by W. H. Roberts, "Proceedings of Seventh General Council, 1899", p. 95.

than on any nation on earth, or than *on no nation*." Washington said in May, 1776: " When I took command of this army (June, 1775) *I abhorred the idea of independence.*" " The first voice raised in America ", says Bancroft, " to destroy all connection with Great Britain came from the Scotch-Irish Presbyterians." [39] The first Declaration of Independence, certainly the first body of resolutions to that effect, was sent forth by the Mecklenburg Assembly, in session at Charlotte, North Carolina, composed of twenty-seven stanch Calvinists, of whom nine were Presbyterian ruling elders and one a Presbyterian preacher.

The deciding voice in Congress. When, twelve months later, Jefferson's Declaration was submitted to the Continental Congress, and that body hesitated and wavered, Dr. John Witherspoon, a Presbyterian preacher, the only clergyman in the Congress, the only minister of Jesus Christ whose name is graven on the pedestal of a civic statue on the American soil, arose and gave the deciding voice. " There

[39] " Hist. U. S.", vol. x. p. 77.

is a tide ", he said, " in the affairs of men. We perceive it now before us. To hesitate is to consent to our own slavery. That noble instrument should be subscribed this very morning by every pen in this house. Though these gray hairs must soon descend to the sepulchre, I would infinitely rather that they descend thither by the hand of the executioner than desert at this crisis the sacred cause of my country." John Witherspoon was a lineal descendant of John Knox.

Witherspoon's spirit was shared by the whole body of American Presbyterians. So intense, universal, and aggressive was their zeal for liberty that the struggle of the colonists for independence was spoken of in England as " The Presbyterian Rebellion ". An ardent colonial devotee of King George wrote home: " I fix all the blame of these extraordinary proceedings upon the Presbyterians. They have been the chief and principal instruments in all these flaming measures. They always do and

" The Presbyterian Rebellion."

145

ever will act against government from that restless and turbulent anti-monarchial spirit which has always distinguished them everywhere." [40]   When news of " these extraordinary proceedings" reached England, Horace Walpole said in the English Parliament, " Cousin America has run off with a Presbyterian parson ".

The brunt of the struggle. When war's thunders and lightnings began to roll and flash, the Presbyterians breasted the storm.   " The members of that Church ", says the author of the sixth volume of " American Church History ", " bore the brunt of the struggle for independence from the Hudson to the Savannah." [41]   Their military enthusiasm was like that of one of their own preachers, who, when the patriots' wadding gave out in a fight close by his church, rushed into the building,—but let Bret Harte tell the story:

[40] " Presbyterians and the Revolution ", p. 49.
[41] p. 69.

146

THE CREED TESTED BY ITS FRUITS

> They were left in the lurch
> For the want of more wadding. He ran to the
>   church,
> Broke the door, stripped the pews, and dashed out
>   in the road
> With his arms full of hymn-books, and threw down
>   his load
> At their feet. Then above all the shouting and shots
> Rang his voice : ' Put Watts into 'em ; boys, give 'em
>   Watts.'
>
> "And they did. That is all. Grasses spring, flowers
>   blow
> Pretty much as they did ninety-three years ago.
> You may dig anywhere, and you'll turn up a ball,
> But not always a hero like this ; and that's all."

At Kings Mountain, where " the aspect *Victory of* of the war was changed and Cornwallis left *the Shorter* no choice but to retreat ",[42] all six of the *Catechism.* colonels in command save one were Presbyterian elders, and their troops were mustered from Presbyterian settlements. When we remember that Generals Morgan and Pickens, who won the equally pivotal battle of the Cowpens, were also Presbyterian elders, and that after his surrender at Saratoga, Burgoyne said to Morgan concerning

[43] " Bancroft's Hist. U. S.", vol. x. p. 340.

his Scotch-Irish riflemen: " Sir, you have the finest regiment in the world "; when we remember that " more than one half of the officers and soldiers of the American army were Presbyterians," [43] we can understand the statement of Dr. Elliott, editor of the Western organ of the Methodist Church, that " in achieving the liberties of the United States the Presbyterians of every class were foremost ", and appreciate Dr. Hodge's remark that the Shorter Catechism fought through successfully the war of American Independence.

Education.   Had we space we could show how our boasted common-school system is indebted for its existence to that stream of influence which flowed from the Geneva of Calvin,[44] through Scotland [45] and Holland, to Amer-

[43] " Westminster Anniversary Addresses ", p. 30.
[44] See Chap. II. p. 96.
[45] " Knox returned from Geneva fully impressed with the conviction that the education of the masses

ica, and how for the first two hundred years of our history almost every college and seminary of learning, and almost every academy and common school was built and sustained by Calvinists. Says Gen. John Eaton, LL.D., Ex-United States Commissioner of Education: " The Presbyterians by universal consent stand for intelligence."

We could show what an immeasurable influence the Presbyterian Church has exerted upon the national character through the superlative emphasis it has ever placed upon those two sacred institutions on which depend the purity and the permanence of our nation's life, the Sabbath and the Family. As Dr. Landrum, an eminent Baptist minister, said recently at Atlanta: " It is the conservator of the most valuable principles. It has the soundest scholarship. All denominations look to Presbyterianism for a wise leadership in all that pertains to *The Sabbat and the Family.*

is the strongest bulwark of Protestantism and the surest foundation of a state." " The Puritan in Holland, Eng. and Am.", vol. ii. p. 19, note.

the preservation of the Lord's Day, and to
the preservation of the Family."

Benevolence.   We could show how pre-eminently great
and rich have been the streams of benevolence by which the Presbyterian Church
has blessed our own and other countries
through its unequalled power to develop in
its members the character-elements that
command success and the consecration that
makes that success tributary to the service
of God and our fellow men. On this point
the Rev. Robt. M. Patterson, D.D., LL.D.,
says, concerning the American Presbyterian Church: "The simple fact is, that, absolutely and relatively, Presbyterians stand
far in advance of any other denomination.
About half of all the moneys raised by all
the churches of the land for benevolent
work is raised by them." [46]

[46] "American Presbyterianism" (1895), p. 120.
"Benevolent work" does not include the moneys
raised by each individual church for its own con-
gregational purposes. In a certain pure sense of
that word these may be regarded as selfish rather
than benevolent contributions.

THE CREED TESTED BY ITS FRUITS

We could show from history how nearly *Revivals of*
all the far-spreading continental reforma- *religion.*
tions and revivals of religion, which from
time to time have blessed not only America
but Christendom, have been of Calvinistic
origin, after the type of that first great
Christian revival in Jerusalem under Peter,
whose preaching embodied such bold Calvinism as " Him, being delivered by the determinate counsel and fore-knowledge of
God, ye have taken and by wicked hands
have crucified and slain." (Acts 2: 23.)

We could show how incalculable has *National*
been the service rendered the nation by the *leadership.*
Presbyterian Church through its peculiar
ability to develop moral and intellectual
manhood, and thus fit men for responsibility and leadership. Prof. Baldwin of the
Yale Law School pronounces the Presbyterian " the most American Church ",
and Mr. Gladstone says she develops a
" genuine individuality; the love of law
combined with the love of freedom." The
power and prominence of Presbyterians in

civic and national life is so out of proportion to their numbers that the secular press
has made it a matter of sharp and wondering comment. "In calling the roll of the
great men of this nation," says Dr. Newell
Dwight Hillis, "the number of Presbyterian presidents, of legislators and jurists,
of authors and editors, teachers and merchants, has been vastly disproportionate
to the membership of the Church."[47] The
Presbyterian precedence he justly describes
as " this unique pre-eminence." Ambassador Bayard recently declared that Presbyterianism stands for the best element of
American greatness. Mr. Moody, whose
shrewd views of men were only matched
by his unexampled opportunities for observation, said of the Presbyterian Church:
" That Church has the brains of the United
States."[48] To such expert testimony to
the moral and intellectual pre-eminence
of Presbyterians may be added the state-

[47] " Westminster Anniversary Addresses ", p. 254.
[48] Id., p. 314.

ment, made some years ago by the greatest religious weekly of the world, that while the Presbyterian Church was not the largest, few would deny it the name of the leading religious denomination of America.

The above facts of history and observation we have set forth, not to stimulate denominational vanity, but to fill us with gratitude to God for that past history and that present eminence which should be to every one of us

"A vantage-ground for nobleness";

above all to kindle in our hearts a holy enthusiasm for that Divine system of truth, which, under God, has been the foremost factor in the making of America and the modern world.

153

IV

THE CREED ILLUSTRATED

" As for you ye thought evil against me, but God meant it unto good."—Gen. 50: 20.

IV

THE CREED ILLUSTRATED

We shall illustrate Calvinism and the Calvinistic point of view by a brief discussion of the twin doctrines of Predestination and Providence.

God is Sovereign. He reigns Supreme *Predestina-* in fact as well as in right. This universe to *tion and* Him is not a surprise, a defeat, a failure, but *Providence.* a development of His eternal purpose. That purpose is Predestination. That development is Providence. The one is the all-wise predetermined plan in the mind of God; the other is the all-powerful execution of that plan in the administration of the universe.

Says an able commentator and divine: " Calvinism, tho' it is often represented

157

Method of Divine government. as a mere system of doctrine or of abstract dogmas having no practical bearing, is, in fact, a system of government—a method and form in which the Divine power is put forth in the administration of the affairs of the universe. It is based on the idea that God rules; that He has a plan; that the plan is fixed and certain; that it does not depend on the fluctuations of the human will, on the caprice of the human heart, or on the contingencies and uncertainties of undetermined events in human affairs. It supposes that God is supreme; that He has authority; that He has a right to exercise dominion; that for the good of the universe that right should be exercised, and that infinite power is put forth only in accordance with a plan."

God has a plan. To suppose that God ever acts without a plan, in a purposeless, random way, is an impossible conception of the Divine character. How does even a wise man act? He first determines upon the end he desires to attain, and then upon the best means of attaining it. Before the architect begins his edifice, he makes his drawings and forms his plans, even to the minutest details of construction. In the architect's brain the building stands complete in all its parts before a stone is laid. So with the merchant, the lawyer, the farmer, and all rational and intelligent men. Their activity is along the line of previously formed purposes, the fulfilment, so far as their finite capacities will allow, of preconceived plans. Our common sense, therefore, teaches us that in His government of this world which He has made, God is sure to have His own definite purposes in view, and His own definite plans by which He will secure their fulfilment.

It is also evident that these Divine purposes and plans must include not some but all events, " whatsoever comes to pass ",[1] otherwise there would be some things coming to pass which He had not designed or expected or counted on—which is incredi

God's plan all-embracing.

[1] Shorter Catechism, Question 7.

159

ble, and which might defeat the purposes He had formed in reference to other things —which is equally incredible.

The control of the greater must include the control of the less, for not only are great things made up of little things, but history shows how the veriest trifles are continually proving the pivots on which momentous events revolve. The persistence of a spider nerved a despairing man to fresh exertions which shaped a nation's future. The God Who predestinated the course of Scottish history must have planned and presided over the movements of the tiny insect that saved Robert Bruce from despair.

God is no absentee Deity, sitting outside the universe and seeing only the events that lift themselves like peaks above the common level. He is " everywhere present ",[2] " upholding, directing, disposing, and governing all creatures, actions, and things, from the greatest even to the

[2] Larger Catechism, Question 7.

least." [3]   The affairs of the universe are controlled and guided, how? "According to the purpose of Him Who worketh all things after the counsel of His own will." [4] His all-embracing purpose or "decrees", says the Catechism, "He executeth in the works of creation and providence." [5] That is to say, Providence is God's execution of His decrees; in other words, it is simply God's universal and certain fulfilment of His predetermined purposes.

While illustrations of this truth crowd the *Story of Scriptures*, there is one inspired biography *Joseph.* which holds and will ever hold the gaze of mankind, because in that life above any other recorded in history the presiding mind of God and the guiding hand of God are not only felt, but distinctly traceable. The story of Joseph is a picture in miniature of the Divine method of government painted for us by the hand of inspiration. Here we

[3] "Confession of Faith", Chap. **V** section 1.
[4] Eph. 1 : 11.
[5] Shorter Catechism, Question 8.

have Foreordination made familiar, **and** Providence made palpable.

Illustration.   In the 42d chapter of Genesis we see the ten sons of Jacob, driven by stress of bitter famine into a foreign country, and there prostrating themselves before their unknown brother, the all-powerful governor of the land, and dependent upon him for the means of life.   Was this pre-eminence of Joseph over his brethren a mere accident of fortune?   Did it just happen so?   On the contrary, it was distinctly foretold by God to Joseph's family twenty-two years before through those two prophetic dreams of the eleven sheaves and the eleven stars that did him obeisance.   It was simply the fulfilment of God's predetermined purpose, a fulfilment not through miracles, but through the orderly march of His Providence.

Illustration.   In the 37th chapter we see the lad Joseph in the hands of his murderous brothers and begging with tears for his life.   They refuse.   They determine to kill him outright at once. At Reuben's suggestion they change their minds and decide to starve him to death in a pit. Reuben disappears, intending to return when his brethren have gone and rescue Joseph and restore him to his father. In his absence a merchant caravan passes by on its way to Egypt. They change their minds again and at Judah's suggestion determine to sell him as a slave to these traders. This they do and Joseph is carried off to Egypt. Was the result of all these purposes and cross-purposes and changes of purpose accidental? Not so. That result was foreordained of God to fulfil a merciful purpose of His. As Joseph said twenty-two years later to his penitent brothers: "It was not you that sent me hither but God, for God did send me before you to preserve life, to preserve you a posterity in the earth and to save your lives by a great deliverance."[6] Thus Joseph's going to Egypt, though apparently fortui-

[6] Gen. 45 : 5, 7.

tous, was but the fulfilment of a Divine purpose, a fulfilment not through miracle, but through the natural workings of Providence.

Illustration. In the 46th chapter we see Joseph sending wagons for his father's household, and the whole family, with all their wives and little ones, moving down into Egypt and settling in the land of Goshen. This removal to Egypt is the culmination of an extended series of events, most of which appear entirely fortuitous. Jacob's partiality to Joseph leads to his brethren's hatred; their hatred leads to his being sold to Potiphar in Egypt; the wickedness of Potiphar's wife leads to his imprisonment; his imprisonment leads to his acquaintance with the royal butler; this acquaintance leads to his presentation to Pharaoh; his service to Pharaoh leads to his exaltation over all Egypt to prepare for the famine; the famine drives his brethren down into Egypt to seek food from the hand of his power; his power enables him to transport the entire family to Egypt and give them a home in the richest part of the land.

We see, then, that the settlement of Jacob's family in Egypt was the result of a long and complicated chain of events, which a hundred chances might have broken at a hundred points, the whole forming to human eyes what we are accustomed to call a fortuitous concurrence of circumstances. But was there anything fortuitous? Nay, verily. Every link of that chain was forged by the hand of God Himself to bring about that very result, and that result was the fulfilment of a Divine purpose which God had revealed to Abraham two centuries before, the purpose, viz., to make Egypt the training school of His chosen people. Long before any of the present actors were in existence, before a child was born to Abraham, God had said to him: "Know of a surety that thy seed shall be a stranger in a land that is not theirs, and shall serve them, and they shall afflict them four hundred years, and also that nation whom they shall serve will I judge; and afterward shall they come out with great substance." [7]   So we see that these intricate happenings that issued in the migration to Egypt were but the orderly fulfilment by Providence of God's predetermined purpose.

The above Scripture narrative is but an inspired illustration of how God governs the world always and everywhere.   The God of Providence is the same yesterday, to-day, and forever.

Foreordination and fatalism.   The doctrine of our Standards is not that " whatever must be, must be ", but that whatever God has decreed and purposed shall be.   The one expression attributes the course of events to a blind mechanical necessity, the other to the intelligent purpose of a personal God. The one is fatalism, the other Foreordination, Predestination, Providence.   The Bible does not say " whatever must be, must be ".   It says:

[7] Gen. 15 : 13, 14.

"That *that is determined* shall be done." [8]
It says again: "The Lord of hosts hath
sworn, saying, 'Surely *as I have thought,*
so shall it come to pass; and *as I have purposed,* so shall it stand.'" [9] It reveals to us
the glorious truth that our human lives and
our sensitive human hearts are held, not in
the iron cog-wheels of a vast and pitiless
Fate, not in the whirling loom of a crazy
Chance, but in the almighty hands of an infinitely good and wise God.

How God can be sovereign and yet man *Foreordina-*
be free, how God as Supreme Ruler can de- *tion and free*
cree events beforehand and bring them to *agency.*
pass exactly as decreed without interfering
with the freedom of the human agent, is a
question man cannot answer. But God
can. God knows how to govern the natural world by fixed laws, the brute creation
according to their instincts, and human beings agreeably to their natures. By the Divine decree "neither is violence offered to

[8] Dan. 11 : 36.
[9] Is. 14 : 24.

167

the will of the creatures, nor is the liberty
or contingency of second causes taken
away, but rather established." [10] And the
perfect harmony between Foreordination
and free agency which we cannot explain
in our theories we can plainly see in God's
practice.

Illustration. For example, Jacob's preference for Joseph, the wise and good child of his beloved
Rachel, above the ten coarse and brutal sons
of Leah, Bilhah, and Zilpah, was the natural prompting both of his judgment and
his heart. Here is free agency; but here
also is Foreordination; for this partiality, as
the result showed, was the first step in the
fulfilment of God's plan for saving thousands of human lives.

Illustration. Joseph's brethren hate him and sell him
into slavery, seeking to carry out the free
and unconstrained impulses of their jealous
and wicked hearts; and the Ishmaelite merchants are naturally delighted to secure a
young and handsome slave for a mere trifle.

[10] " Confession of Faith ", Chap. III, section 1.

Here is free agency, attested in the con-
science-smitten cry: " We are verily guilty
concerning our brother "; but here also is
Foreordination; for these people, while free
agents, were also so entirely God's agents
that the Scripture says it was God that
" *sent* Joseph into Egypt to preserve life ".

Potiphar's wife was free in seeking to *Illustration*
carry out first her lustful and then her re-
vengeful impulses toward Joseph; the royal
butler was free in carrying out his courtier-
like impulses toward Pharaoh; Pharaoh
was free in carrying out his humane and
statesmanlike impulses toward his famine-
threatened nation; Joseph was free in
carrying out his filial impulses in sending
for his beloved father. Here in each case
was the most unquestionable free agency;
but here also was the most unquestionable
Foreordination; for the result of it all was
the exact fulfilment of a purpose which God
had revealed to Abraham two centuries before, that not Canaan but fertile and civil-

ized Egypt should be the nursery of the chosen people.

Illustration. In the Mediterranean the vessel carrying Paul to Cæsar at Rome is caught in a violent storm and driven helpless and half-sinking before the unceasing fury of the tempest. God says to Paul: " Fear not; thou must be brought before Cæsar, and behold I have given thee all them that sail with thee."[11] Here is the Divine decree,— All shall be saved. Shortly after, as the sailors are secretly preparing to escape in the boat from the doomed ship, Paul says to the centurion and soldiers: " Except these abide in the ship, ye cannot be saved." [12] Here is free agency and the efficiency of second causes, liberty in the midst of certainty, a human will that *can*. The soldiers cut the boat adrift; the vessel is wrecked, but all escape safe to land. Here are two undeniable facts: " All shall be saved "; " Except these abide in the

[11] Acts 27 : 24.
[12] Acts 27 : 31.

ship, ye cannot be saved." Here are two co-operating factors, Divine Predestination and human free agency. It was God's purpose to save all lives on the ship. It was Paul's purpose to use the human means within his reach. God has a purpose and is at work. Paul has a purpose and is at work. And the result of the forces correlated and co-working is the saving of all on board, the exact fulfilment of the Divine decree.[18]

In that dread yet glorious drama of hu- *Illustration* man sin and redeeming love which culminated on Calvary, we see the human actors moving on the stage influenced by human motives, exercising their freedom of will, and responsible for what with "wicked hands" they do. Caiphas, Judas, the priests, Herod, Pilate, all act according to the self-promptings of their various natures. We hear their consultations, their agreements, and disagreements. We see

[18] Pitzer's " Predestination, God's Working Plan of His Universe ", p. 12.

their stratagems, their plans, their changes of plan. Human forces—pride, bigotry, curiosity, envy, covetousness, and malice— are in fullest, freest, most abandoned play. Yet every step and every act of every actor had not only been preordained, but predicted, and the judgment of the Holy Ghost is given in these solemn words: " Him *being delivered by the determinate counsel and foreknowledge of God*, ye have taken, and by wicked hands have crucified and slain." [14] " For of a truth against Thy holy Child Jesus, whom Thou hast anointed, both Herod and Pontius Pilate, with the Gentiles and the people of Israel, were gathered together, *to do whatsoever Thy hand and Thy counsel determined before* (Revised Version, *foreordained*) *to be done*." [15]

" The secret things belong unto the Lord our God." God's Foreordination, therefore, we cannot doubt. Neither can we doubt the foreordained freedom of the moral creature. This freedom is asserted or assumed on

[14] Acts 2 : 23.
[15] Acts 4 : 27, 28.

172

every page of Scripture. It is emphatically declared in our Standards. It is loudly proclaimed by the universal consciousness of mankind. Here are two impregnable facts: God's Predestination and man's eternally predestinated freedom. Though the problem of their reconciliation is insoluble to our finite sin-beclouded minds, ignorant as we probably are of some of the essentials of the problem, and incapable as we undeniably are of appreciating the significance of the Infinite Factor involved, yet it is clear from Scripture and history that the problem presents no difficulty to God. Reason, religion, and philosophy alike require us to accept both facts, denying neither, abating the force of neither, " holding to the Divine efficiency without flinching, making our faith stout and masculine with it; holding equally to human accountability, making our faith elastic and agile with it "; and as to the harmony between them, we may leave it and leave it cheerfully, till we stand on higher summits in a clearer light.

Providence and sin.

Overhung with a mystery impenetrable as yet to human eyes is the relation of the Divine Providence to human sin. Our Standards are careful to guard the character of God from any aspersion in view of the dread mystery of evil. They teach that God cannot be tempted with evil, neither tempteth He any man. They refer sin immediately to the "freedom and power to do that which is good",[16] originally given to man as a moral creature. Of all sinful acts whatsoever, they affirm with emphasis that "the sinfulness thereof proceedeth only from the creature and not from God, Who, being most holy and righteous, neither is nor can be the author or approver of sin."[17]

Sinful acts included in God's plan.

That sinful acts, however, are included in God's plan is a truth abundantly evident in Scripture.

"Saul took a sword and fell upon it."[18]

[16] "Confession of Faith", Chap. IX, section 2.
[17] Id., Chap. V, section 4.
[18] I Chron. 10: 4.

174

It was his own wicked act. Yet it fulfilled a Divine purpose revealed years before concerning David; it executed Divine justice; Scripture speaks of it as the punitive act of God Himself. " So Saul died for his transgressions which he committed against the Lord. And he inquired not of the Lord; therefore He slew him and returned the kingdom unto David the son of Jesse." [19]

The act of his brethren in selling Joseph into Egypt was an evil act. Yet it formed an integral part of God's plan. It was intended to produce the most beneficial results. " As for you ", said Joseph to his brethren, " ye thought evil against me, but God meant it unto good to bring to pass as it is this day, to save much people alive." [20]

There never was a more evil act than that of those who

> "slew the Lord,
> And left their memories a world's curse."

" By wicked hands ", says the Scripture, He was crucified and slain. Yet it was " by

[19] I Chron. 10 : 13.
[20] Gen. 50 : 20.

175

the determinate counsel and foreknowledge of God ".

Supremely wicked was the conspiracy
that contrived His death, yet the conspira-
tors " were gathered together to do whatsoever Thy hand and Thy counsel determined before to be done ".

"The Lord reigneth; let the earth rejoice." Did we believe that so potent and fearful
a thing as sin had broken into the originally
holy order of the universe in defiance of
God's purpose, and is rioting in defiance of
His power, we might well surrender ourselves to terror and despair. Unspeakably
comforting and strengthening is the Scriptural teaching of our Standards [21] that be-
neath all this wild tossing and lashing of

[21] "Confession of Faith", Chap. V, section 4. "The
almighty power, unsearchable wisdom, and infinite
goodness of God, so far manifest themselves in His
providence, that it extendeth itself even to the first
fall, and all other sins of angels and men, and that
not by a bare permission, but such as hath joined
with it a most wise and powerful bounding, and
otherwise ordering and governing of them, in a mani-
fold dispensation, to His own holy ends; yet so, as
the sinfulness thereof proceedeth only from the creature", etc., etc.

evil purposes and agencies there lies, in mighty and controlling embrace, a Divine purpose that governs them all. Over sin as over all else, God reigns Supreme. His Sovereign Providence " extendeth to the first fall and all other sins of angels and men ", so that these are as truly parts and developments of His Providence as are the movements of the stars or the activities of unfallen spirits in heaven itself.[22] Having chosen, for reasons most wise and holy though unrevealed to us, to admit sin, He hath joined to this bare permission a " most wise and powerful bounding " of all sin, so that it can never overleap the lines which He has prescribed for its imprisonment, and such an " ordering and governing " of it, as will secure " His own holy ends ", and manifest in the final consummation not only His " almighty Power " but His " unsearchable Wisdom " and His " infinite Goodness ".

[22] Morris's " Theology of the Westminster Symbols ", p. 223.

Grand truth grandly stated.

Thus we rise to the height of that sublime, eternal, all-comprehending decree and plan of God, to fulfil which " He doth uphold, direct, dispose, and govern all creatures, actions, and things, from the greatest even to the least, by His most wise and holy Providence, according to His infallible foreknowledge, and the free and immutable counsel of His own will, to the praise of the glory of His wisdom, power, justice, goodness, and mercy." [23]

Transfigures nature.

Upon the material universe this mighty doctrine sheds a transfiguring radiance. It consecrates every branch of physical science. The student of nature in tracing out her laws and processes feels with Kepler that he is " thinking the thoughts of God after Him ".

Glorifies history and human life.

From this faith there falls a yet greater glory upon the history and life of man. It invests them with a Divine significance. It relates them to the eternities past and to come. The obscurest task in life is en-

[23] " Confession of Faith ", Chap. V, section 1.

nobled by the thought that it is a thread in the warp and woof of that Divine purpose at which we are ever weaving in the ceaseless loom of time.

It is a doctrine unspeakably precious to *Most comforting.* the Christian heart amid the storms and darkness of this earthly pilgrimage—to know that every trial, every burden, every bereavement, every sorrow has been foreseen and foreappointed by a wisdom that cannot err and by a love that cannot change,

> " That every cloud, that spreads above
> And veileth love, itself is love."

Instinctively in its sorrow the heart clings to this faith, feeling that in fatherly kindness the affliction was foreordained, for reasons wise though unknown, and saying in trust, though it be in tears, not, " It is chance; it is ill-fortune ", but " It is the Lord, let Him do what seemeth Him good ". "For we know that all things work together for good to them that love God, to them who are the called according to His purpose." [24]   And this blessed purpose of good the next verse declares: " For whom He did foreknow He also did predestinate to be conformed to the image of His Son."

Most energizing.   The most comforting and ennobling is also the most energizing of faiths.   That its grim caricature, fatalism, has developed in human hearts an energy at once sublime and appalling is one of the commonplaces of history.[25]   The early and overwhelming onrush of Mohammedanism, which swept the East and all but overthrew the West, was due to its devotees' conviction that in their conquests they were but executing the decrees of Allah.   Attila the Hun was upborne in his terrible and destructive course by his belief that he was the appointed " Scourge of God ".   The energy and audacity which enabled Napoleon to attempt and achieve apparent impossibilities was

[24] Rom. 8 : 28.
[25] T. V. Moore's " Power and Claims of a Calvinistic Literature ", p. 10.

nourished by the secret conviction that he was " the man of destiny ". Fatalism has begotten a race of Titans. Their energy has been superhuman, because they have believed themselves the instruments of a superhuman power.

If the grim caricature of this doctrine has breathed such energy, the doctrine itself must inspire a yet loftier, for all that is energizing in it remains with added force when for a blind fate, or a fatalistic deity, we substitute a wise, decreeing God. Let me but feel that in every commanded duty, in every needed reform, I am but working out an eternal purpose of Jehovah; let me but hear behind me, in every battle for right, the tramp of the Infinite Reserves; and I am lifted above the fear of man or the possibility of final failure. I am inspired with a Divine strength and confidence. So in former chapters we have seen how in the long struggle for human advancement, civil and religious, wherever the surge of battle has rolled fiercest and

fastest and the day of toil has hung hottest
and heaviest, there always have been found
the holders of this faith. Rooted in the
Divine Word, this doctrine has borne
through all the ages heroes and martyrs
innumerable. Against them, as against
Joseph, have been used all the weapons
that rage and hate could devise. But
in dungeons, in dens and caves of the
earth, on battle-field, rack, and scaffold,
they were more than conquerors. For they
knew with a victorious confidence, that not
Satan, or chance, or fate, but God was Sovereign; that even the wrath and wickedness of men were but carrying out His eternal purpose; and that the day was surely
coming when to all these hostile agencies
they could say, as Joseph said to his brethren: " As for you, ye thought evil against
me but God meant it unto good."

APPENDIX

It may interest our readers to learn that
the Calvinistic view of nature and life,

which was derived exclusively from the
Scriptures, is in striking harmony with
modern scientific philosophy and with the
ascertained facts of history and observation. Regarding the grounds of the Divine
choice, Matthew Arnold, the trained student of life and history, whose sympathies
were not with Calvinism, frankly says: "In
rebutting the Arminian theory the Calvinists are in accordance with historical truth
and with the real march of human affairs."[1]
The historian Froude, himself held by no
trammels of sect or party, unhesitatingly
affirms that "Calvinism is nearer to the
facts, facts which no casuistry can explain
away."[2] With a different nomenclature,
and a different idea of the truth of super-
naturalism, the foremost modern scientific
philosophers hold the Calvinistic world-
view. Mr. Froude cites as examples John
Stuart Mill and Mr. Buckle. With equal
appositeness he might have named Mr.

[1] "St. Paul and Protestantism", p. 21.
[2] "Short Studies on Great Subjects", pp. 11, 12.

Herbert Spencer, Mr. Lecky, Prof. Huxley, and many more. Sadly as these may diverge on the question of God's rational will and free personality, extremely as their necessitarian metaphysics may conflict with the true doctrine of His Providence and grace, their impression of the co-ordinated facts of observation is thoroughly Calvinistic.

We submit upon this point the compact yet luminous statement of the celebrated Dr. Abraham Kuyper, Professor in the University of Amsterdam, Member of the States General of Holland, and one of the profoundest of living thinkers. " It is a fact ",[3] he says, " that the more thorough development of science in our age has almost unanimously decided in favor of Calvinism with regard to the antithesis between the unity and stability of God's decree, which Calvinism professes, and the superficiality and looseness, which the Arminians preferred. The systems of the great

[3] " Lectures on Calvinism ", p. 149.

modern philosophers are almost to one in favor of unity and stability. Buckle's ' History of the Civilization in England' has succeeded in proving the firm order of things in human life with astonishing, almost mathematical, demonstrative force. Lombroso, and his entire school of criminalists, place themselves on record in this respect as moving on Calvinistic lines. And the latest hypothesis, that the laws of heredity and variation, which control the whole organization of nature, admit of no exception in the domain of human life, has already been accepted as ' the common creed' by all evolutionists. Though I abstain at present from any criticism either of these philosophical systems or of these naturalistic hypotheses, so much at least is very clearly demonstrated by them, that the entire development of science in our age presupposes a cosmos, which does not fall a prey to the freaks of chance, but exists and develops from one principle, according to a firm order, aiming at one fixed plan. This

185

is a claim which is, as it clearly appears, diametrically opposed to Arminianism, and in complete harmony with Calvinistic belief, that there is one Supreme will in God, the cause of all existing things, subjecting them to fixed ordinances and directing them towards a pre-established plan. As a Calvinist looks upon God's decree as the foundation and origin of the natural laws, in the same manner also he finds in it the firm foundation and the origin of every moral and spiritual law; both these, the natural as well as the spiritual laws, forming together one high order, which exists according to God's command, and wherein God's counsel will be accomplished in the consummation of His eternal, all-embracing plan."

V

THE CREED CATHOLIC

"Endeavoring to keep the unity of the Spirit in the bond of peace. There is one body, and one Spirit, even as ye are called in one hope of your calling; one Lord, one faith, one baptism, one God and Father of all."—Eph. 4: 3-5.

V

THE CREED CATHOLIC

The catholicity of Presbyterianism,[1] its liberality of thought and feeling, its freedom from sectarian narrowness and bigotry, is one of its crowning characteristics. Benjamin Harrison, that noble gentleman, statesman and Christian, whose death our whole country still mourns, said with truth: "There is no body of Christians in the world that opens its arms wider or more lovingly to all who love the Master than the Presbyterian Church."

The catholicity of Presbyterianism is no mere sentiment. It is not a thing of individual profession or platform declamation. It is rooted in our creed. It is proclaimed

Our Standards catholic

---

[1] The words "catholicity" and "catholic", as used by the author in this chapter, have no reference to the Church of Rome.

in our Standards. It is embodied in our doctrine of the Church. "The visible Church", says our Confession, "consists of all those throughout the world who profess the true religion together with their children." [1] Thus formally and publicly do we repudiate the name of "the" church and claim only to be a church of Jesus Christ. Not only do our Standards contain no denunciation of the antagonistic views of sister evangelical churches, they are said to be the only church Standards in existence which make explicit and authoritative recognition of other evangelical churches as "true branches of the Church of Jesus Christ." [2] To the "Communion of Saints", our Confession devotes an entire chapter. We are there taught that our "holy fellowship and communion" in each other's gifts and graces, in worship and mutual service of love, "is to be extended

[1] "Confession of Faith", Chap. XXV, sec. 2.
[2] "Book of Church Order", Chap. II, sec. II, par. ii.

unto all those who in every place call upon the name of the Lord Jesus." [3]

The catholicity of our Standards finds *Recognition* beautiful expression in the Presbyterian *of other churches.* attitude toward all sister evangelical churches. While a branch of evangelical Christendom unchurches all sister denominations, such action is abhorrent to Presbyterian feeling and unknown to Presbyterian practice. Members and ministers of other evangelical churches we treat as in all respects true members and ministers equally with ourselves of the Church of Christ.

While several of these churches decline giving letters of dismission from their own to other communions, we make no distinction. We dismiss members to Baptist, Episcopal, or other Christian congregations, in precisely the same form, and with the same affectionate confidence, as though we were transferring them to churches of our own name.

[3] "Confession of Faith", Chap. XXVI, sec. 2.

Some evangelical denominations deny the validity of ordinances performed by sister churches, and when a minister or a member would come to them from a sister denomination, the one must be re-ordained, the other re-baptized. Such denial is utterly contrary to the Presbyterian spirit and usage. We never repeat the rite. The ordinance of a sister church we accept as no less valid than if performed by ourselves.

While from many evangelical pulpits the ministers of sister churches are shut out, or from co-officiation in sacred ceremonies, such exclusion is never practiced by us. It is alien to the Presbyterian heart and habit. We are as free and cordial in asking Episcopal, Baptist, or other evangelical ministers, to occupy our pulpits, or assist us officially in administering the Lord's Supper, as in asking our own pastors.

We unchurch no true Christian. We reject no ministerial ordination. We repudiate no administered scriptural sacrament of a sister church. Returning good for evil, we recognize our high-church fellow clergyman as a true minister of Christ, and our immersionist brother as having been validly baptized. We respond with all our hearts to the "Amen" of the Methodists; we join with our brethren in any psalmody that puts the crown upon the brow of Jesus; and most lovingly do we invite our fellow Christians of every name and denomination to partake with us of the emblems of His broken body and His shed blood. We have no prejudice, no peculiarity, no crotchet of any kind, to restrict our Christian sympathies and dig a chasm between us and other servants of our Master. Our catholicity is wide as evangelical Christendom. When the day of union dawns upon the militant forces of our common Lord, and His prayer is answered "that they all may be one", it will be largely due under God to the teaching and the example of the Presbyterian Church.

The catholic breadth of her Christian sympathy is seen in her liberal support

*Support of
unsectarian
institutions.* of interdenominational and undenomina-
tional religious enterprises and institutions
of all kinds. Wl.erever the common cause
of Christ calls for the sacrifice of sectarian
interests and the submergence of sectarian
differences, the Presbyterian Church is ever
first to respond, with greatest gifts and
largest labors. She stands with hand out-
stretched and purse open for every needy
worthy cause that bears the name of Christian. Her members have been called
" God's silly people " from the self-forget-
ful generosity with which they have lav-
ished the time and means often sorely
needed by their own church upon those
great outside enterprises whose sole claim
is the common Christian good and whose
sole appeal is to the catholic Christian
heart. The statement of D. L. Moody is
well known, that if he needed one hundred
thousand dollars for some worthy unde-
nominational religious enterprise, he would
naturally expect to secure eighty thousand
of it from the Presbyterians. In the great

interdenominational societies and associations, and in those private or public charities sustained by the gifts of good people of all Christian names, figures show that Presbyterians usually *do* and *give* not only more than any other denomination, but often more than all the others combined.

In a western city the Young Men's Christian Association was seeking funds to secure a new building. After sixty thousand dollars had been given by one Presbyterian, a general committee of one hundred was appointed, representing all denominations. That number proving too large for effective work, a special canvassing committee of five was selected, taken from the leading business men, and limited to those who would contribute at least five thousand dollars. Four of these so appointed were found to be Presbyterian elders. The Young Men's Christian Association Secretary said that this was about the proportion in other cities.[4]

Young Men's Christian Association.

American Bible Society.   The American Bible Society is one of the noblest unsectarian institutions in the world. Its beneficent work eternity alone can measure and reveal. Dr. S. Irenæus Prime, the genial and famous author and editor, was corresponding secretary of the Society. A few years before his death he made a careful examination of the receipts of the New York City Bible Auxiliary. He found that for the preceding fifty years the contributions to the Society from the Presbyterian churches were five times greater than the sum total from all the other churches combined, and for the preceding seven years were six times greater. Dr. Prime adds that " an analysis of the sources of contributions to the Bible cause in any other city or part of the country, out of New England, will show that the Presbyterian Church contributes to this great national Society in about the same proportion." [5]

The American Bible Society, the Amer-

[5] " First General Presbyterian Council ", p. 70.

ican Tract Society, and the American Sunday School Union are our three national religious enterprises, the importance of whose work, and the utterly unsectarian character of whose management and aims, commend them equally to all Christians. One of the leading executive officers of one of these Societies, himself not a Presbyterian, said that if the Presbyterian Church should withdraw its contributions and cooperation from any or all of these Societies, their great work would thereby be ended.[6]

American Tract Society and S. S. Union.

The above facts and figures illustrate the nobly practical nature of the catholicity of the Presbyterian Church. She issues no formal declarations concerning unity,

"For love hath better deeds than words to grace it."

She simply practices that catholic Christian bigheartedness which her Bible and her Standards teach.

Her catholic spirit of love finds beautiful expression in the administration of her magnificent philanthropies. In the North-

Catholic philanthropy.

[6] Hays' "Presbyterians", p. 353.

ern Presbyterian Church alone there are more than a dozen Presbyterian Hospitals, Homes, Orphanages, and the like, for the care of the needy and the relief of the suffering. They are completely equipped, and the inmates of the hospitals enjoy the benefits of the highest medical skill and the best attendance which money can command. These noble institutions represent an outlay of millions on millions of Presbyterian money, but they are Presbyterian only in their support and management, not in the objects which they seek to relieve. Their arms are stretched forth to receive and bless all, without regard to name or creed. In one of these hospitals, seventy-four in every hundred of the inmates came from the Methodists, the Catholics, and the Lutherans, while only eight were Presbyterians. The Jews, Unitarians, and Friends helped to make up the rest.[7]

The catholicity of the Presbyterian Church appears in her one condition of

[7] Hays' "Presbyterians", p. 352.

church membership. She demands nothing *One condition of church membership.* whatever for admission to her fold except a confession, uncontradicted by the life, of faith in the Lord Jesus Christ. The applicant is not asked to subscribe to our Standards or assent to our theology. He is not required to be a Calvinist, but only to be a Christian. He is not examined as to his orthodoxy, but only as to his " faith in and obedience unto Christ." [8] He may have imperfect notions about the Trinity and the Atonement; he may question infant baptism, election, and final perseverance; but if he trusts and obeys Christ as his personal Saviour and Lord, the door of the Presbyterian Church is open to him, and all the privileges of her communion are his.

When churches prescribe conditions of membership other than the simple conditions of salvation, they are guilty of the unscriptural incongruity of making it harder to get into the Church than into Heaven.

[8] "Confession of Faith", Chap. XXVIII, sec. 4.

To such ecclesiastical tyranny and exclusiveness the Presbyterian Church stands in utter contrast. Her Standards declare that as simple faith in Christ makes us members of God's family,[9] so " those who have made a profession of faith in Christ are entitled to all the rights and privileges of the Church." [10] Thus with a broad and beautiful catholicity the gates of our Presbyterian Zion are flung wide as the gates of Heaven for all the children of God.

Magnifies the essentials. The Presbyterian Church is catholic in its embrace and emphasis of those great essentials of the Christian religion which form the common faith of evangelical Christendom. The central facts of redemption, which are at once the heart and the life of the Christian system, to wit, that Jesus Christ is very God and very man, God manifest in the flesh, the one only power unto salvation from sin and endless death

[9] " Ye are all the children of God by faith in Jesus Christ." Gal. 3 : 26.
[10] ' Book of Church Order", Chap. III, sec. 3.

by atoning expiatory sacrifice, through
faith alone, these, with the other fundamen-
tal doctrines believed by all Christian communions throughout the world, are held by
the Presbyterian Church with a grasp that
none can loosen and preached with a power
that none can dispute. In her Standards
and her pulpits they receive, as they de-
serve, the supreme emphasis and honor.

Even those articles of her creed which *The Presby-*
some suppose distinctive are more catholic *terian the*
than denominational. In her practice of in- *catholic*
fant baptism she is in harmony with nine *creed.*
tenths of Christendom. In her mode of
baptism she stands again with the overwhelming majority of Christendom. In
her doctrine of election, predestination,
and final perseverance she is in line with the
majority of the historic creeds of the evangelical world. It is hardly too much to say
that if, from all the authoritative articles of
belief of the various churches, one were to
make a choice, selecting only such beliefs
as are held by the whole or the largest

part of evangelical Christendom, the elect and catholic creed so formed would correspond, almost doctrine for doctrine, with the creed of Presbyterians.

Dr. Briggs quoted.

Says Dr. Charles A. Briggs: " Presbyterianism is pre-eminently Christian." [11] " The Presbyterian Church has the true apostolic succession in striving after the apostolic faith in its purity, integrity, and fulness." [12] " Presbyterianism is a real Christianity which rejects everything that is not a product of the Christianity of Jesus Christ. It appropriates everything in every age of the Church which bears the impress of Christ and which represents the power of His Spirit." [13] " The Presbyterian churches adhere to all the doctrinal achievements of the ancient church—the catholic doctrines of the Trinity, the Person of Christ, and the

[11] " American Presbyterianism ", p. 5.
[12] Id., p. 8.
[13] Id., p. 11.

office of the Holy Spirit. They do not adopt the peculiarities of the Greek or the Roman or any other branch of the Christian Church, whether in doctrine or practice; for these peculiarities are not catholic. Presbyterianism is truest to catholicity in that it insists upon those things which are truly catholic, and declines to mingle with them those things which are not catholic." [14]

"Presbyterianism", declares the same writer, "belongs to the modern age of the world, but it is not a departure from the Christianity of the ancient and mediæval church. It is rather the culmination of the development of Christianity from the times of the apostles until the present day. It comprehends the genuine Christianity of all ages. It conserves all the achievements of the Christian Church. It leads the van of the advancing host of God. It makes

" The genuine Christianity of all ages."

steady progress towards the realization of the ideal of Christianity in the golden age of the Messiah." [15]

Liberal in non-essentials.

The stress laid by the Presbyterian Church upon the essentials of religion is the secret of her liberality in non-essentials. The vestments of the minister, the attitude of the worshipper, the precise order and form of worship, and the like, she leaves to the Christian common sense of the individual church. Regarding such matters she may advise or recommend. She never legislates. She is ever mindful of her Lord's prayer, " Sanctify them *through Thy truth* ". An exaggerated illustration of the Presbyterian indifference to things about which we have no commandment from the Lord is the exclamation of a noble old Scotch elder when sounded on the burning question whether or not his minister should wear a gown: " Let him attend to his own wardrobe; he may preach in his shirt-

[15] " American Presbyterianism ", p. 5.

sleeves for aught I care, if he only preaches sound doctrine."

Our Presbyterian polity, or form of *Our polity* church government, whence comes the de- *scriptural.* nominational name we bear,[16] is derived from Scripture. The famous Anglican scholar and prelate, Bishop Lightfoot, candidly declares: " It is a fact now generally recognized by theologians of all shades of opinion that, in the language of the New Testament, the same officer in the church is called indifferently bishop or elder or presbyter."[17] Says Prof. Heron of Belfast: " It is a simple historical fact, of deep significance, that wherever the Reformation had free course, wherever it was permitted to shape itself spontaneously after Scripture, and without external interference, it assumed a Presbyterian form." Among the young Protestant Churches of native growth to-day, which are struggling

[16] We are Presbyterians, because our churches are governed by presbyters (or elders or bishops). Every elder is a bishop according to the New Testament.
[17] Com. on Philippians.

into life amid the Romanism of Southern Europe, the Mohammedanism of Western Asia, the superstitions of Brazil, or the heathenism of Japan, the same tendency is seen, the same process is going on.[18] As soon as the initial stage of Congregationalism is outgrown, there begins the grouping into Presbyteries, the natural and scriptural flowering into the complete Presbyterian form.

Unequalled. That the Presbyterian is the best church polity, as the London *Spectator* unhesitatingly affirms, would appear not only from its scriptural origin, but also from the fact that its principles of popular representative government have been adopted by all the most enlightened nations of the earth.

Growingly universal. While the scripturalness and excellence of our ecclesiastical polity are familiar themes, few properly recognize its growingly catholic and universal character. The Presbyterian polity is rapidly leaven-

[18] Ogilvie's "The Presbyterian Churches", p. 158.

ing all the Protestant churches. It is working visibly in every sister denomination.
Only the repressing hand of the State in
Germany to-day prevents the Lutheran
Church from adopting a Presbyterian constitution. The Lutherans of America have
adopted synodical government as the best
suited to their needs, and have associated
the representatives of the people with their
pastors in their local and national councils.
The earlier Anglican prelacy has given way
in America to a distinctly Presbyterian
type of Episcopal government. The English Episcopal Church has adopted synodical rule in all her colonial branches, where
in her synods layman and cleric meet together with the Bishop as permanent Moderator.[19] The Methodists have been
obliged to modify their clerical government
by the admission of lay members to their
conferences. Modern Congregationalism
is a manifest compromise between the Independent and the Presbyterian way. Even

[19] Ogilvie. p. 161.

the Baptists, who have been the stanchest representatives of Independency, have come to intrust the real management of denominational affairs to local and national associations, the former treating churches which walk disorderly as liable to the discipline of exclusion from the association.[20]

"Presbyterian in substance."

The above are some of the approximations on the part of the sister Protestant churches to methods formerly peculiar to Presbyterianism. The able author of the sixth volume of " American Church History " states that " As a whole the Protestantism of America has become Presbyterian in substance, though not in name." [21] When comes that day for which many are longing and praying, when the churches of Protestant Christendom shall abandon their isolation and unite in one mighty Evangelical Federation, there can be little doubt that its form, and the chief factor in its formation, will alike be Presbyterian.

[20] " American Church History ", vol. VI. p. 285.
[21] Id., p. 285.

THE CREED CATHOLIC

The catholic and ecumenical character of *Number of adherents.* Presbyterianism is proved and pictured in the numerical vastness of her constituency. Her adherents are variously estimated at from twenty-five to forty millions.[22] Rev. W. W. Moore, D.D., LL.D., says: " The Presbyterian Church is the largest Protestant church in the world to-day." Rev. R. P. Kerr, D.D., the historian of Presbyterianism, pronounces it " by far the largest Protestant church on the globe ". Rev. Moses D. Hoge, D.D., LL.D., *nomen clarum et venerabile,* said from his pulpit: " The largest Protestant family in the world is the Presbyterian."

It is inspiring to remind ourselves that *"Be ye followers of them who through faith and patience inherit the promises."* ours is a historic church. Our present millions are the children and successors of millions upon millions more, seated now in the galleries of " History's vast Coliseum ",

[22] Dr. W. H. Roberts' estimate is twenty-five millions, Dr. J. N. Ogilvie's twenty-eight millions, Dr. W. A. Campbell's thirty-one millions, Dr. James McCosh's thirty-four millions, Dr. R. P. Kerr's thirty-five millions, Dr. W. P. Breed's forty millions.

tier above tier, generation upon generation, of those who through ages of toil,
trial, and triumph, " subdued kingdoms,
wrought righteousness, obtained promises,
stopped the mouths of lions, quenched the
violence of fire, out of weakness were made
strong, waxed valiant in fight, turned to
flight the armies of the aliens ".   When we
remember that as Presbyterians we stand
on soil drenched with the blood, baptized
with the tears, and eloquent of the achievements of saints and heroes in number without number, surely our hearts should cry
out, in language sacred as familiar: " *We*
cannot dedicate, *we* cannot consecrate, *we*
cannot hallow this ground.   The brave men
who struggled here have consecrated it far
above our power to add or detract.   It is
for us the living rather to be dedicated here
to their unfinished work."   " In the memory of their mighty acts ", says Dr. W. M.
Paxton, " we should train our children.
The historian Sallust tells us that the Roman mothers trained their children in the

presence of the busts and statues of their ancestors. In like manner we should train our children and our rising ministry, as it were, in the presence of their forefathers, in all the memories of our past history, and urge them, as the Roman mothers did, never to be satisfied whilst the virtues and victories of the past were more numerous or more glorious than those of the present."

More catholic and imposing even than the Presbyterian numbers is the worldwide range of the Presbyterian empire. While the adherents of other Protestant communions are more or less massed in single countries, the Lutherans in Germany, the Episcopalians in England, the Methodists and Baptists in the United States, the line of the Presbyterian Church is gone out through all the earth. She thrives this hour in more continents, among a greater number of nations and peoples and languages, than any other evangelical church in the world. As her witnesses in continental Eu-

Worldwide empire.

rope, she has the historic Presbyterian Reformed churches of Austria, Bohemia, Galicia, Moravia, of Hungary, Belgium, France, Germany, of Italy, Greece, the Netherlands, of Russia and Switzerland and Spain. She is rooted and fruitful in Africa, in Australia, in Asia, in Great Britain, in North America, in South America, in the West Indies, in New Zealand, in Malanesia,—the people of this faith and order gird the earth. Presbyterianism possesses a power of adaptation unparalleled by any other system. It holds in steadfast array a great part of the intelligence and moral vigor of the Christian world, and from its abounding spiritual life are going forth the mighty forces of Christian missions into all the heathen world.

" Go ye into all the world."

On every continent, on the islands of the sea, on the soil of every non-Christian faith, Presbyterianism has planted her standards. Eager to break the bread of life to the perishing, and reveal to the restless darkened millions " that Light whose dawning maketh all things new", she has gone out, as her Master bade, through the lands near at hand, on and on, unto the uttermost parts of the earth.

No other church in America has ex- *Missionary* tended its banners and flung out its line of *aggressive-ness of* battle as the American Presbyterian Church *American* has done.[23] In this respect at least the *Presbyterian-* belief of Dr. C. A. Briggs seems justified, *ism.* that "American Presbyterianism is in advance of all other Christian denominations in the realization of the ideal of Christianity."[24] The missionary heralds of our Pan-American Presbyterianism alone, which is but a branch of the Catholic Presbyterian Church, are scattered from British Columbia to Yucatan; they are in Central America, and in Colombia, Venezuela, British Guiana, and Brazil; they are on the African coast from Liberia to the Ogowe, and in the heart of the great Congo Basin; they are strong in Syria and Persia, and side by

[23] Robt. E. Speer.
[24] "American Presbyterianism", p. xiii.

side in India our separate columns are advancing under one Captain; we are proclaiming glad tidings in Siam and Laos, in Hainan and the Philippines, in Cuba and Formosa; we have long since " partitioned China ", not for political spoil, but for her own salvation; our united forces are teaching the Hermit Nation that as no man, so no nation, liveth to itself; we have proclaimed to the Sunrise Kingdom the Sun of Righteousness, whose rising shall know no setting. Our strategic points are taken, our stations occupied, our watch-towers girdle the globe.[25]

The outlook. With a past rich in glorious achievement and a present marked by worldwide extension and triumphing missionary enthusiasm, the future of the Presbyterian Church is radiant with promise. Who can doubt that through historic development, through centuries of special experience, through stern battles with relentless ene-

[25] Report of Com. on For. Missions, Western Section, to Seventh General Council.

mies as well as through the silent sweeter
nurture of His love, God has constituted
our Presbyterianism one of His elect
agencies in the fulfilment of that gracious
Purpose which includes not ourselves only,
but the whole world? May He thrill us
with the consciousness of our Divine com-
mission and endowment. May He give us
grace, with an humble reliance on His en-
abling Spirit, to do our part in that great
and blessed work, whose aim is the universal enthronement of our common Lord,
and whose end is nothing less than the re-
generation of humanity.

INDEX

Alva, 76

AMERICA, Calvin and founding of, 119, 132–136; Calvinism and colonial elements of. 120; Calvinism and republican principles of, 121, 122, 126–130; Calvinism the training school of, 120, 137; national constitution modelled after Presbyterian, 140–142; summary of Calvinism's contributions to, 142; the Revolution a Presbyterian, measure, 143–148; work and influence of Pres. Church in, 148–152

American Bible Society, 196

American S. S. Union, 197

American Tract Soc., 197

Anglo-Saxondom, its Protestantism due to Puritans, 72; Calvin's influence upon, 131

Apostolic Succession, 202

Aristotle, 33

Arminianism, 92, 94, 183, 184, 186

Arnold, Matthew, cited, 94, 183

Arnold, Thomas, cited, 15

Assembly, see General Ass., or Westminster Ass.

Attila, 180

Augustine, 13, 87

Bacon, Francis, 16, 33

Bacon, Dr. Leonard Woolsey cited, 120

Baldwin, Prof., cited, 151

Bancroft, cited, 72, 78, 81, 82, 90, 91, 96, 121, 122, 127, 129, 130, 136, 143, 144

Baptism, not repeated, 192; infant, 201; mode, 201

Baptist approximation to Presbyterianism, 208

Baptist Association, cited, 36

Baxter, 17, cited, 18

Bayard, Ambassador, cited, 152

Bayne, Peter, cited, 64

Beecher, H. W., cited, 47, 62

Benevolence, 150

Bible-readings, 110

Bishop, in New Test. usage, 205

Book of Ch. Order, cited, 190

Bowen, Dr. L. P., cited, 61

Breed, Dr. W. P., cited, 146, 209

Briggs, Dr. C. A., cited, 31, 202, 203, 213

Bruce, Robert, 160

Buckle, cited, 92, 98, 102, 121, 183, 185

Bunker Hill, 135

Bunyan, 17, 59

CALVIN, not originator of Calvinism, 12; C. and Pres. creed, 13; and Catechisms, 25; and Scripture, 33; and God, 47;

INDEX

INDEX

Free-agency and foreordination illustrated, 167–172; both to be believed, 172, 173

Froude, cited, 43, 57, 58, 59, 60, 72, 99, 125, 183

General Assembly, Southern, cited, 15; Northern on revision of Confession, 37, 38; Southern and revision, 38; Archbishop Hughes on, 139

Geneva, 55, 130, 131, 135, 136

German Reformed Church, 120, 212

Gibbon, 58

Gillespie, George, 29

Gladstone, cited, 151

"God's silly people," 194

Green, J. R., cited, 20, 47, 65, 73, 74, 122, 128, 129, 141

Gunsaulus, F. W., cited, 120

Hampden, 17

Harrison, Benjamin, cited, 189

Harte, Bret, cited, 147

Hays, Dr. Geo. P., cited, 195, 197, 198

Heath, Richard, cited, 138

Heidelberg catechism, 27

Henry, Matthew, 17

Heresy, hostile to Calvinism, 11

Heron, Prof., cited, 205

Hillis, Dr. N. D., cited, 152

History vs. fiction, 60

Hodge, Prof. A. A., cited, 148

Hoge, Dr. M. D., cited, 209

Holland, Calvinists of, their sufferings and heroism, 75–77; by what inspired, 78; leader, 78; morality, 79; achievements, 80–82; intellectual freedom, 91; contributions to America, 120, 143

Home, the Christian, created by the Puritan, 73; a Scotch Presbyterian, 106–116

Hospitals, Presbyterian, 198

Howe, John, 17

Hughes, Archbishop, cited, 139

Huguenots, character, 83–86, product of Calvinism, 86; in America, 120, 143

Hume, cited, 125

Huxley, cited, 184

Independent, The, cited, 70

Infants dying in infancy, 39

Ironsides, 71

James, King, cited, 129

Jansen, 87

Jefferson, Thomas, cited, 143

Joseph, story of, illustration of Predestination and Providence 161–175

Kepler, 178

Kerr, Dr. R. P., cited, 209

King's Mountain, battle of, 147

Knox, chief aim, 47; character, 59; pupil of Calvin, 98, 130; creator of Scotland, 99; effect of his teaching, 122, 123

Kuyper, Prof. Abraham, 184

Landrum, Dr., cited, 149

Larger Catechism, completed before Shorter, 26; cited, 160

Law of God, Confession's chapter on, 22

Leadership, national, 151

Lecky, cited, 63, 84, 184

Leyden, siege of, 76; University of, 97

Liberty, civil, saved to the

220

INDEX

world by Puritans, 71; fruit
of Calvinism, 122–137
Lightfoot, Bishop, cited, 205
Lincoln, Abraham, quoted, 210
Lombroso, cited, 185
Longevity, Puritan, 89
Lord's Prayer, and Calvinism, 45
Lowell, J. R., cited, 47, 73, 104
Luther, 25, 27, 59, 135
Lutheran approximation to Presbyterianism, 207
Lycurgus, 130

Macaulay, cited, 64, 66, 67, 68, 69, 70
Mayflower, 135
McCosh, James, cited, 209
McFetridge, N. S., cited, 55, 85
Mecklenburg Assembly, 144
Melville, Andrew, 59, 122
Methodist approximation to Presbyterianism, 207
Methodist Ecumenical Conference, cited, 12; Conference Wesleyan, cited, 36; Conference, cited, 54
Michelet, Jules, cited, 47
Mill, John Stuart, cited, 183
Milton, 17; cited, 18; 59
Missions, American Presbyterian, 213; and Calvinism, 100, 101
Mitchell, Dr. A. F., cited, 23
Mohammedans, 180
Moody, D. L., cited, 152, 194
Moore, Dr. T. V., cited, 105, 180
Moore, Dr. W. W., cited, 209
Morgan, Gen., 147
Morley, John, cited, 56, 66, 94, 102
Morris, Dr. E. D., cited, 177
Motley, cited, 55, 76, 78, 79, 81, 126, 133, 134

Murray, Regent, 59

Napoleon, 53, 80
New England Puritans, character, 89, 90; example of Calvinistic spirit of free inquiry, 91
Novelists vs. historians, 60

Ogilvie, J. N., cited, 206, 207, 209
Ordination, doctrinal requirements at, 14; not repeated by Presbyterian Church, 192
Owen, John, 17
Paton, John G., 107
Patterson, Dr. R. M., cited, 150
Paxton, Dr. W. M., quoted, 210
Penn, William, 81
Pickens, Gen., 147
Pilgrim Fathers, 91
Pilgrim's Progress, 112
Pitzer, Dr. A. W., 171
Plato, 33
Polity, Presbyterian (see under Presbyterian Church).
Port Royal, 88
PREDESTINATION, in Encyclopedia Britannica, 62; illustrated, 162–176; P. and Providence, 157; and common sense, 158, 159; and fatalism, 166; and free-agency, 167–173; practical effects of, 56, 178–182 (see Foreordination, Providence).
PRESBYTERIAN CHURCH, name, 205; the martyr church, 11, 54; leading representative of Calvinism, 12; doctrinal church, 14; condition of membership, 14, 199; of ordination, 14; Scripture's champion and mar-

221

INDEX

Selden, John, 28

Shakespeare, 15

SHORTER CATECHISM, Assembly's last and best work, 26; definition of God, 30; first question strikes keynote of Calvinism, 45; safeguard against error, 49; effect on Scottish peasantry, 101; in the home, 110; in the Revolution, 148, cited, 45, 159, 161

Smiles, Samuel, cited, 85, 86, 91

Smith, Goldwin, cited, 66

Solon, 130

Sovereignty, Divine, 44; and William the Silent, 78; illustrated, 157-182

Spectator, London, cited, 206

Speer, R. E., cited, 213

Spencer, Herbert, cited, 184

Standards, see Westminster Standards.

Stanley, Dean, cited, 19

Stanley, Henry M., cited, 100

Stephen, Sir James, cited, 128

Strickler, Dr. G. B., cited, 27

Subscription formula, 14

Taine, cited, 47, 65, 68, 69, 153

Ten Commandments, catechisms' exposition of, 22, 49

Thompson, Dr. R. E., cited, 146, 208

Tilghman, Chief Justice, cited, 142

Twisse, Dr William, 17

Ursinus, 25

Walpole, Horace, cited, 146

Washington, George, cited, 144

Watts, Isaac, 17

WESTMINSTER ASSEMBLY, name and era, 15; personnel, 16; estimates of, 18, 19; background, 19; task, 21; first characteristic, thoroughness, 24-28; advantages and training, 24, 25; second characteristic, prayerfulness, 28-31; third characteristic, loyalty to Scripture, 32-36

WESTMINSTER STANDARDS, doctrinal, 13; and church membership, 14; and office-bearers, 14; formula of subscription to, 14; name and era of formulation, 15; ethical quality, 21; spiritual vitality, 22; use and function, 21, 23; labor and prayer bestowed upon, 24-31; scripturalness, 32-36; and philosophy, 33; hard sayings in, 34; why assaulted, 35, 36; Calvinism of, unimpaired by past or proposed revision, 37, 38. (See Catechisms, Shorter, Larger; Confession.)

William the Silent and Calvinism, 78; father of religious liberty, 81

Wilson, Dr. S. Law, cited, 61

Witherspoon, Dr. John, 144

Young Men's Christian Association, 195